Management

f-LAWS

How organizations really work

Russell L. Ackoff

& Herbert J. Addison

with considered responses by
Sally Bibb

Published in this first edition in 2007 by:

Triarchy Press
Station Offices
Axminster EX13 5PF
United Kingdom

+44 (0)1297 631456
info@triarchypress.com
www.triarchypress.com

ISBN   0-9550081-2-3
        978-0-9550081-2-2

Cover design by:
Tim Heap – www.logomotion.co.uk

Foreword

It is delightful to find how much wisdom Russ Ackoff and Herb Addison have packed into a few *f*-Laws. But it shouldn't have been a surprise. I've been reading Russ Ackoff's work for fifty years and it is never less than pithy, even when the format is more academic than in this present book.

There is nothing precious about Russ's gurudom, and his commitment to diversity in viewpoints is as sincere as it gets. So it was no surprise that these distinguished authors were prepared to have their wisdom scrutinised by someone younger and less well-known; Sally Bibb is, in my view, someone to watch out for – a forward-thinker and an excellent communicator.

Diverse views are a great antidote to blinkered thinking. The contrast in this book, across the generations, across the Atlantic and across the gender divide is a perfect example of complementary dialogue, a resource we ought to see used a lot more in organizations.

I recall Russ Ackoff's lively columns in the journal *Systems Practice* in the 1990s. One of these was entitled 'The Corp. Jester'. He wrote:

> *"Medieval royal courts had court jesters who unfortunately disappeared even when the courts remained. They should be reincarnated and placed in corporate courts… Corp. jesters must be able to ask questions that others either have not thought of, or dared to ask. In addition, they must be able to provide answers that are not expected, even by the 'kings' before whom they perform."*

So, corporate royalty, wherever you are, please read this book, learn its lessons and act on them, if you wish your kingdoms to endure.

Gerard Fairtlough

Introduction

At first sight, *Management f-Laws* needs no introduction. You need only glance at one or two of the *f*-Laws to get the picture of Russell Ackoff's ironic and often subversive take on how organizations *really* work, not how they *think* that they work. These epigrams are unspoken laws and unconventional wisdoms of management exposed to full daylight as the management flaws they actually are. Some *f*-Laws are downright funny; others bemuse; all provoke in one way or another. At worst, they elicit denial or anger. At best, they evince recognition followed by a desire to think profoundly about the inevitability of change. And thus, the need to know *how* to change.

Management f-Laws is one of those books that can grace the coffee table in the reception area. It won't be out of place on the bedside table. But it should most definitely be on your desk. Dip into it, and on any of its pages you will find something to laugh or argue about but, above all, to take on board.

Making us laugh is its most obvious strength. But it is bound to be a lot more than funny, for Russell Ackoff has been around for a long time and, when it comes to organizations, he knows what he is talking about. At the grand age of 87, he is known internationally for his pioneering work on Systems Thinking. He continues to rank highly in the list of the Top 50 Business Brains and is affectionately known to many in the Systems Thinking community as the 'Dean'. Ackoff's work in research, consulting and education has involved hundreds of corporations and many governmental agencies in the US and abroad. He has authored or co-authored 20 books and published over 150 articles. He has taught hundreds of leaders, aspiring managers and Systems Thinkers the meaning of learning.

A quick look at Systems Thinking

For those unfamiliar with Systems Thinking and Design, it is worth considering why it is relevant to the world of work. First, Systems Thinking recognises that organizations are made up of people doing things together, and that all activities have an effect on what happens to the parts *and* the whole. It asserts that systems are dynamic, complex and interactive. Second, Systems Thinking says that the component parts of a system behave differently when they are seen as part of the whole compared to when they are isolated from each other or from their environment. This debunks the traditional approach to problem solving in which the problem is analysed in isolation. Unless you look first at the whole, and the interaction between all the parts, isolated analysis won't help: understanding the links and interactions between the elements that comprise a whole system is crucial. What Systems Thinking focuses on is the importance of organizational communication at, and between, all levels.

In a world increasingly dominated by notions of complexity and globalization, Systems Thinking offers another way of thinking about how we work. For an organization to succeed, managers must look beyond departmental functions and targets, and learn about the effect of their activities on the corporate whole and the interaction between its parts as well as on stakeholder organizations. Executives need to be flexible, creative and, above all, responsive to rapid change. They need to be leaders who embrace complexity.

Systems Thinking, Change and Management f-Laws

All this may seem pretty obvious. But Russell Ackoff, and his co-author, Herbert Addison, believe that we, as managers, claim to know all this but don't act on it. For them, the best way to get us to take Systems Thinking on board is through a subversive presentation of how we *really* work in organizations. For them, the way most organizations work *is* the way of the f-Law – a series of unspoken laws of management behaviour. Ackoff and Addison have written:

> "these simple management truths are widely held precisely because they are simple yet very important. They guide managers' everyday behavior much more than the fundamental, but complex, truths revealed by scientists, economists, politicians, or philosophers. The truths these wise thinkers reveal are at most frosting on the cake. The truths presented here are the cake."

How to read this book

The f-Laws are not presented in any particular order. As a collection of subversive epigrams, *Management f-Laws* shows us how organizations really work, in order to provoke thought about how to improve them. Learn the wisdom of the *f*-Law, and you will start thinking better and differently. Change won't be a breeze, but it will be a challenge to relish. Dip into the book and on any page you may recognise your boss, your company or your own hidden pathology. Read the explanation of each *f*-Law and you will start to think about why it is important to learn how to change – your attitudes, your practices, your values.

Take any *f*-Law: consider whether the flawed behaviour applies to you, your subordinates, part of your organization, all of it, or the interaction between its parts. The effect, for example, of a hierarchical tradition, such as the seemingly innocuous executive restroom (*f*-Law 22), when worked through Ackoff's Systems Thinking, may reveal that segregation of the workforce in that place signals a dislocation of all the parts of the organization. Ask yourself where else this kind of hierarchy is practised. Is there a lack of communication between divisions as well as between the people in them? The boundaries that were designed to maintain order may, in fact, incubate dysfunction.

Management f-Laws is not a prescription *for* change but a provocation *to* change. Don't read it from cover to cover. Take it in small bites. For as Professor Wladimir Sachs writes:

> "A lifetime of thinking about management and experiencing its arcane rituals is summarized in the form of f-Laws, making for very entertaining reading. But make no mistake: this is a fun way of going about serious work. Each of the laws hits hard on common sins of management, and should be taken by the reader very personally as a stimulus to think 'out of the box' about what really matters."

Sachs told me that he has seen Ackoff on many occasions "*torture executive groups with much coarser versions of the f-laws*", in order to provoke them into doing just that. His suggestion to read an *f*-Law at the start of every meeting is a good one. Ackoff's Management *f*-Laws get you thinking 'out of the box'. They make you want to change and to change creatively and effectively.

<u>Why have a response to the *f*-Laws?</u>

Part of Ackoff's incitement to change involves the permission, demand

and necessity to question each *f*-Law, to test it against your own experience and to come up with different, and better ways to make those changes. To that end, we invited Sally Bibb, specialist in organizational development and author of the recently published *The Stone Age Company*, to read this collection of *f*-Laws and to make a spontaneous, if considered, response to them. In the true spirit of critique, Sally pitches her views with verve and aplomb.

In the process of editing this project, we came to understand why she was such a good choice. She comes at organizational change from a different but associated perspective. Where Ackoff speaks of organization as a system made up of parts, which, if you want to make changes, need analysing as a whole, Bibb concentrates on understanding people in organizations in order to look for ways to help them work more effectively. Sally is a pioneer and she practises what she preaches in her work. Her work at The Economist Group empowers her to use her experience as well as her training in organizational change. It keeps her very much in touch with the world of international business. In all of this she brings together the relational, the inspirational and the qualities required to lead. It is her profound understanding of individual learning and the learning organization that allows her to inspire people in her writing.

Few businesses last more than a few years. There is no prescribed solution to this state of affairs. *Management f-Laws* helps us realise that it is the small flaws, as well as the big ones, that cause businesses to falter. Bibb has taken note of how few companies manage to inspire passion, enthusiasm and loyalty in their workers. The ones that do seem to do it spectacularly well; and yet they are still few and far between. She knows that good change-agents are people who connect generously and enthusiastically with others and share their knowledge and resources and inspire others. Conversing with Ackoff and Addison is just one way that she is achieving that goal.

By introducing another voice, the book becomes a conversation through which, as Sachs remarks, the *"thoughtful commentary by Sally Bibb jump-starts one's own reflections"*. Her voice highlights the two-way process of any reading in which the reader has a right to be different. Age, gender and culture inevitably come into play. It's not that Bibb is resistant or antagonistic to Ackoff's approach to change:

she often agrees with him. It is more a difference of emphasis and tone. If Ackoff and Addison talk more about the traditional, large corporation where, one suspects, the notion of pioneer is often absent, Sally accentuates the spirit of leadership, pioneering and the need for trust and cooperation. She is a voice for 'people'. Whilst lurking within Ackoff's sardonic take there is an attitude to learning that spells out that clear, critical thinking is the real indicator of learning, Sally evidences the process. For Ackoff, Addison and Bibb the learning organization is what ƒ-Laws are about.

A final word on voice

For ease of reading, different fonts have been used to distinguish the voices of Ackoff/Addison and Bibb. The ƒ-Law is presented on the left-hand page, the response on the right. The authors' punctuation, it seems to me, reflects something of their respective voices; as does the difference between American and British English spellings. Ackoff's style consciously echoes the carefully honed law plus the philosopher's commentary. Bibb's has a spontaneity and speed that reflects the conversational riposte and the best, creatively driven meeting.

We have chosen to scatter a few of Ackoff's illustrations through the book as, from the outset, the combination of law, commentary and illustration reminded us of C. Northcote Parkinson's *Parkinson's Law* with its illustrations by Osbert Lancaster.

One last word: this introduction has spoken a lot about Russell Ackoff and Sally Bibb. But I have thus far failed to mention the role of Herb Addison in the making of this book. I would say that this is almost inevitable given the man's enormous modesty. So great, in fact, that at one point, he asked to be taken off the title page! But having spent several months working on this project, I know only too well what an enormous contribution Addison has made to each ƒ-Law – something that Russ Ackoff was quick to affirm. He has been the sounding board, the incisive critic and most excellent fine-tuner of the ƒ-Laws and commentaries. His knowledge of business, his editing for Oxford University Press business and management books, but above all, that keen ability to question, analyse and evaluate make him the perfect arbiter of Ackoff's most outstanding ideas.

Rosie Beckham – Triarchy Press

Contents

15. When managers say something is obvious, it does not mean that it is unquestionable, but rather that they are unwilling to have it questioned

16. The less sure managers are of their opinions, the more vigorously they defend them

17. The more lawyers an organization employs, the less innovation it tolerates

18. Good teachers produce skeptics who ask their own questions and find their own answers; management gurus produce only unquestioning disciples

19. The only thing more difficult than starting something new in an organization is stopping something old

20. Acceptance of a recommended solution to a problem depends more on the manager's trust of its source than on the content of the recommendation or the competence of its source

21. The less managers understand their business, the more variables they require to explain it

22. The higher the rank of managers, the less is the distance between their offices and their restrooms

23. Business schools are as difficult to change as cemeteries, and for the same reasons

24. Curiosity is the "open sesame" to learning, even for managers

25. The legibility of a male manager's handwriting is in inverse proportion to his seniority

26. Executives must be prevented from receiving any information about frauds or immoral acts committed by their subordinates

27. There is nothing that a manager wants done that educated subordinates cannot undo

28. The more corporate executives believe in a free (unregulated) market, the more they believe in a regulated internal market

29. The amount of time a committee wastes is directly proportional to its size

30. It is generally easier to evaluate an organization from the outside-in than from the inside-out

31. Development is less about how much an organization has than how much it can do with whatever it has

32. Smart subordinates can make their managers look bad no matter how good they are, and make their managers look good no matter how bad they are

33. In an organization that disapproves of mistakes, but identifies only errors of commission, the best strategy for anyone who seeks job security is to do nothing

34. The best organizational designers are ones who know how to beat any organization designed by others

35. The offence taken by an organization from negative press is directly proportional to its truthfulness

36. The less important an issue is, the more time managers spend discussing it

37. The time spent waiting to get into an executive's office is directly proportional to the difference in rank between the executive and the one waiting to get in

38. Administration, management and leadership are not the same thing

39. In acquisitions the value added to the acquired company is much more important than the value added to the acquiring company

40. Business schools are high security prisons of the mind

41. No matter how large and successful an organization is, if it fails to adapt to change, then, like a dinosaur, it will become extinct

42. The size of a CEO's bonus is directly proportional to how much more the company would have lost had it not been for him or her

43. The less managers expect of their subordinates, the less they get

44. The amount of money spent to broadcast a television or radio commercial is inversely related to its truthfulness and relevance

45. All work and no play is a prescription for low quantity and quality of outputs

46. A bureaucrat is one who has the power to say "no" but none to say "yes"

47. Teleconferencing is an electronic way of wasting more time than is saved in travel

48. The more important the problem a manager asks consultants for help on, the less useful and more costly their solutions are likely to be

49. The distance between managers' offices is directly proportional to the difference between the ranks of their occupants

50. The *sine qua non* of leadership is talent, and talent cannot be taught

51. Managers who don't know how to measure what they want settle for wanting what they can measure

52. A great big happy family requires more loyalty than competence, but a great big happy business requires more competence than loyalty

53. If an organization must grow, it is better for it to grow horizontally than vertically

54. Corporate development and corporate growth are not the same thing and neither requires the other

55. The uniqueness of an organization lies more in what it hides than what it exposes

56. The telephone, which once facilitated communication, now increasingly obstructs it

57. Managers cannot learn from doing things right, only from doing things wrong

58. The principle objective of corporate executives is to provide themselves with the standard of living and quality of work life to which they aspire

59. The principal obstruction to an organization getting to where its managers most what it to be lies in the minds of its managers

60. A corporation's external boundaries are generally much more penetrable than its internal ones

61. It is very difficult for those inside a box to think outside of it

62. The level of organizational development is directly proportional to the size of the gap between where the organization is and where it wants to be

63. Most stated, corporate objectives are platitudes – they say nothing, but hide this fact behind words

64. Most corporations and business schools are less than the sum of their parts

65. Managers who try to make themselves look good by making others look bad, look worse than those they try to make look bad

66. The morality that many managers espouse in public is inversely proportional to the morality they practice in private

67. The higher their rank, the less managers perceive a need for continuing education, but the greater the need for it

68. The number of references and citations in a book is inversely proportional to the amount of thinking the author has done

69. No computer is smarter than those who program it. Those who program computers are seldom smarter than those who try to use their output

70. Managers cannot talk and listen at the same time; in fact, most managers find it very difficult to listen even when they are not talking

71. Overheads, slides and PowerPoint projectors are not visual aids to managers. They transform managers into auditory aids to the visuals

72. Conversations in a lavatory are more productive than those in the boardroom

73. To managers an ounce of wisdom is worth a pound of understanding

74. The press is the sword of Damocles that hangs over the head of every organization

75. The more managers try to get rid of what they don't want, the less likely they are to get what they do want

76. Focusing on an organization's "core competency" diverts attention from its core competencies

77. The greater the fee paid to corporate directors, the less their contributions are likely to be

78. A manager's fear of computers is directly proportional to the square of his/her age

79. Most managers know less about managing people than the conductor of an orchestra does

80. Complex problems do not have simple solutions, only simple minded managers and their consultants think they do

81. When nothing can make things worse, anything can make them better

1. You can't teach an old dog or executive new tricks, or even that there *are* any new tricks.

Most senior executives are relatively near retirement. The less there is of one's future, the smaller is the number of ideas that are seen as new. Eventually, as an executive's professional future approaches zero, there appears to be nothing new under the sun and, therefore, nothing new worth trying. In other words: the future increasingly comes to be perceived as a repetition of the past.

This results in the "We tried it and it didn't work" syndrome. Executives and managers are reluctant to make changes whose effects will not be realized until after their retirement because such changes will have no effect on their reputations and on the bonuses they receive on departure.

This is why most organizational changes occur when there is a change of the corporate guard. In fact, the principal reason for the premature (enforced) retirement of executives is the perception by corporate boards of the need for change.

Unfortunately, it is usually less costly and time consuming in the short run to keep an executive from doing further harm than to hire one who will do some good.

Actually, the other big reason why these executives won't change is that they have too much at stake, i.e. their pensions and perks.

Irrespective of their age or how close they are to retirement most people are simply focused on their own career and its benefits to them. The best executives are focused on doing the right thing. But these are still pretty rare specimens. Plenty of young dogs won't be taught new tricks either.

Young or old: dogs would rather not learn new tricks.

You can't teach an old dog new tricks.

2. Knowledge is of two types, explicit and implicit, and knowing this is implicit.

Explicit knowledge is knowledge that can be consciously captured in manuals, procedural protocols, drawings and plans, and all other codified systems that help in running a business and living our lives. However necessary such knowledge may be it is not sufficient for surviving, let alone thriving. Tacit knowledge is also required.

Tacit knowledge is what individuals and organizations know how to do without thinking. It is done unconsciously. They may be unaware of it or, if aware, may not be able to articulate it, for example, how to ride a bicycle, run, read and write.

The things we do without thinking are more responsible for our survival and welfare than those things we do consciously and deliberately. An objective observer of how we speak, for example, may point out that we use the words "you know" as a type of punctuation. We were not aware of this. But now that we have been made aware of it, we can improve our oral delivery. It is exactly this type of objective observation of what is done unconsciously that a good consultant can bring to an organization's consciousness. For example, in meetings, the participants almost always wait until the most senior member of the group speaks. Then those who follow tend not to disagree strongly with the opinion expressed. Because of this, viable alternatives are not considered. By raising this practice to consciousness the "habit" can be revoked and more significant choices can be considered and made.

Being an effective executive requires flexibility. To be flexible we need to understand the impact we have so we can change what we're doing if it's not getting the result we want. To do this we need self-knowledge and the ability to reflect, learn and change what is not working. To make implicit knowledge explicit we need the skills of learning. Being effective or good at something is of limited use unless we know how we do it. For example, being good at building rapport is generally an unconscious competence. If we know what it is we do that results in good rapport then we can do it consciously when we're in tough situations with people we find difficult.

If you ask someone who is good at something how they do it they will often say, 'I don't know, I just do'. The really excellent ones, like top sportsmen and women, know exactly what they do when they are being successful so that they can repeat it when they need to.

Quite a lot of companies have latched on to coaching. A good coach will help a person discover what it is they are doing that works so that they can repeat it – just as a good sports coach does. But many companies don't understand what good coaches do. They are seen as just another way of embedding skills or sorting out difficult people problems. Good method, poor briefing.

Making the implicit explicit would serve organisations well. It's unlikely to happen soon as executives don't think in this way, and even when they do, they see it as a threat.

3. You rarely improve an organization as a whole by improving the performance of one or more of its parts.

An organization is a system and the performance of a system depends more on how its parts interact than on how they act when taken separately. Suppose the automobile with the best motor is identified, then the one with the best transmission, and so on for each part that an automobile requires. Suppose further that these parts are removed from the cars of which they are a part. Finally, these best parts are assembled into an automobile. We would not get the best possible car; in fact, we would not even get a car because the parts would not fit together, let alone work well together.

Similarly, if each part of a corporation is improved, it does not follow that the organization as a whole will be improved. By improving parts separately, the whole can be put out of business. Evaluation of the performance of parts of an organization should be based first on their effects on the whole, secondly on their individual performance.

In some cases the organizational performance can be improved by reducing the performance of one of its parts: by increasing inventories fewer sales may be lost because of stock shortages. The profit obtained from the otherwise lost sales may be greater than the costs associated with increased inventory. Loss leaders are products sold at a loss in order to induce additional sales of profitable products.

Another take on this is that the performance of the organisation as a whole can be improved if there is improvement in a critical mass. If there are numbers of influential people in the organisation who are improving their ways of working this network can have a powerful effect on the organisation as a whole. It depends who these people are and what they do.

That's why, in theory, change can come from other places than the top. But it takes a canny group of people to realise that.

4. There is no point in asking consumers, who do not know what they want, to say what they want.

Many new product and service introductions have been disastrous despite the extensive surveys conducted to show that there is consumer interest in, and intention to buy, such a product or service. These surveys have incorrectly assumed that most consumers know what they want.

Consumers can discover what they want in products and services by designing them. It is in design that people find what they want. Furthermore, consumer involvement in product/service design almost always gets creative results.

Two examples. A group of men designing their ideal men's store discovered that they did not want the lowest price for clothing of a specified quality but the highest quality for a specified price. (They decided how much they were going to spend before going shopping.) Second, they wanted clothing arranged by size rather than type so they could go to one part of a store where all types of clothing in their size were gathered. (Because they disliked shopping, they waited until they wanted to buy several things before they went shopping.) Third, they wanted saleswomen, not salesmen, because they said, "You can't trust a man's opinion of how you look." Finally, they wanted sales personnel to be available only when asked for.

Then, a group of airline passengers playing with a mock-up of an airplane's interior found out how to arrange the seats so each one was on an aisle, and do so without decreasing the number of seats or increasing the number of aisles.

It's astonishing that focus groups are still the method most organisations (including political parties, of course) use to determine what consumers want.

We know the problems:
- Participants want to impress the people running the group, or to be liked by them
- People's private intentions (never mind their publicly stated ones) seldom match the reality of their behaviour
- Sometimes we lie to ourselves
- We don't know ourselves as well as we think we do

The best organisations are starting to use customers in more and more creative ways – including asking them to design their products. Software companies have been using their best customers to beta-test products for years. Some organisations employ customers on part-time or short-term contracts. The best organisations go further and employ their most vociferous critics. Maybe this is the direction that political parties will go. Already in the UK, the leader of the Conservative Party has hired environmentalist Zac Goldsmith (and a natural enemy of the Tories) to lead his environmental policy group. This ought to work better than the Labour Party's endless focus groups.

5. All managers believe they can do their boss's job better than their boss can, but they forget that their subordinates share the same belief about themselves.

Hierarchy

This and the difference between the salaries of different ranks are responsible for the fact that managers find it easier to look up than down. This enables them to see who is standing on their shoulders but not those on whose shoulders they are standing.

Managers have yet to learn that it is futile to supervise subordinates who know how to do their jobs better than their managers can. Fortunately, smart subordinates can conceal their bosses' ignorance even from their bosses who cannot hear the laughter that comes from behind their backs. Subordinates have yet to learn that no manager's job is as simple as it appears even though many of their managers *are* as simple-minded as they appear.

These issues form part of the bullying culture that is endemic in 'stone-age' organisations that are over-reliant on hierarchical structures, status and orthodoxies. Management in this kind of organisation is about monitoring and controlling the work of others. Many managers believe that they need to be able to do their subordinates' jobs better than they can. Many subordinates believe that too. However, the more complex the work becomes, and the more specialised, the more unrealistic and unnecessary it is to want or expect that.

In the best organisations, people working cooperatively in teams or project groups, sharing the same goals and motivated by leaders and facilitators – not controlled by managers – drive forward to share successes and failures. In this context it's a matter of understanding that responsibility is jointly owned and that cooperation produces mutual rewards.

6. For managers the only conditions under which experience is the best teacher are ones in which no change takes place.

Change, particularly technological change, makes much of what was learned in the past irrelevant or obsolete. Learning how to drive an automobile does not equip one to pilot a space vehicle. Knowing how to work an abacus or slide rule does not equip one to operate a computer.

Experience is no longer the best teacher. Successful management of a corporation in the past provides no assurance of the ability to manage it successfully in the present or future. This is why few corporations live more than twenty years – either going out of business or merging with other corporations. Like corporations, knowledge has a decreasing life span. But unlike corporations, knowledge is easily renewable.

True learning requires openness and humility. The pace of change means that we all have to admit, increasingly often, that there are lots of things we don't know. Yet few managers feel able to say that they don't know the answer. This makes it harder for them to learn. Training courses are full of executives trying to prove how good they are already and how much they know already. (Equally few organisations encourage staff to say they don't know.)

Many organisations think of change and innovation as essential but they lack the ability to make change happen. The best organisational cultures – ones that engender and celebrate learning – are rare, as are leaders who model the ability to admit that they don't have all the answers.

I agree that experience can be over-valued. When a company advertises for someone with ten years' experience, it tends to get someone with a year's experience repeated ten times.

An organisation's inability to learn is one of the most serious problems today. The result is that innovation is cramped by a lack of learning; responsiveness to changes in the market is stunted; and the flexibility to deal with new problems is inhibited. So, let's focus on learning. Companies die because experience is favoured over learning.

7. The level of conformity in an organization is in inverse proportion to its creative ability.

It is difficult, if not impossible, to regiment a creative mind. It tends to violate conventions and traditions without thinking about it. Such violations are means to an end not an end in itself. Creative people often dress peculiarly, even at work, and work at odd hours.

A creative person, unlike a drudge, cannot turn himself or herself off and on easily. Organizations that value creativity must develop tolerance for unconventional behavior. They should realize that such behavior is not a form of protest but a requirement for effective work.

An organization that cannot accommodate nonconformity will not be able to retain creative people. Conformity is a poor substitute for creativity.

This is so obvious. Yet organisations, when they are trying to become more innovative, attempt to do so within the confines of their conformist culture. Creativity flourishes in environments that are the antithesis of most corporative environments. That is exactly why some companies set up innovation labs separately from the main organisation.

We don't tend to think of creativity as something that's necessary for other than the true creative industries such as advertising. But actually all companies these days need their employees to be creative in the way they do their job. Creativity is not just about coming up with big ideas, it's about being able to think about new ways of doing things or new things to do. Everyone can be creative in small ways that can have a positive impact. But they have to know that they are allowed to, that the organisation they work for truly encourages that. What's more, they have to be confident that their company will tolerate mistakes because inevitably, when trying new and different ways of doing things, some will work and some will not.

8. The best reason for recording what one thinks is to discover what one thinks and to organize it in transmittable form.

Corollary: **The principal reason for reading what another thinks is to discover what the reader thinks.**

Preparation of a document should be treated as a learning, not a teaching, experience. The amount that a document can teach its readers is proportional to the amount of learning the author experienced in preparing it.

There is nothing capable of being understood that cannot be expressed in ordinary English. Documents that are not written in ordinary English are not understood even by their authors.

Jargon is wool pulled over a mind to conceal its ignorance from itself. Unfortunately, obscurity is no protection against plagiarism, nor is ignorance.

Writing about or teaching something is a great way to learn about it. To teach something you need to really understand it, to really understand it you need to get under the skin of it and organise your thoughts so that you can impart it to others articulately. I love the notion that the amount that a document can teach its readers is proportional to the amount of learning the author experienced in preparing it. Stephen King in his book **On Writing** says that, if you want your reader to be surprised, as the writer you have to be willing to surprise yourself.

Plain English is a skill that is sadly lacking in most organisations. Learning how to write clearly and plainly is not just a writing skill, it's a lesson in empathy and understanding. Good writers write for readers and not just for the pleasure of writing. They try to understand their readers. The result is the ability to influence because no one can influence us unless we feel that they have some understanding of us. If only organisations and business schools would cotton on to that they might just see an increase in business.

9. No corporation should retain a business unit that is worth more outside the corporation than inside it.

Corporations are supposed to create wealth. To retain an organization that would be worth more on the outside is to destroy wealth, not create it. The only justification for a corporation's owning a business unit lies in the value it adds to that unit. If it fails to add value to the unit or if it adds less value than others can, the corporation does society a disservice by retaining it.

Parts of a corporation should be free to emigrate, and encouraged to do so, when they believe that doing so would increase their value. The existence of such a right would make corporations more aware of their responsibility to increase the value of their parts to others if not to themselves.

The right to emigrate is the most important freedom an individual or organization can have. It provides the strongest incentive for preserving the other rights that define freedom.

This sounds like a very altruistic notion. I've never come across a corporation with that attitude.

Corporations tend to treat their individual parts like they treat their employees; the emphasis is not on what the corporations can do for them, it's what they can do for their employers. The whole notion of 'contribution' as one of the measures of success is evidence of the fact. Contribution is amongst the measures used in a company to value its businesses. Performance appraisal is the mechanism by which they judge their employees. There is no reverse mechanism by which the corporation's return support is valued.

A huge shift in thinking about what a corporation is for and how it should create value for society at large would be required. And, of course, that's exactly what we need. But these big philosophical questions tend not to occupy the minds of chief executives. Where there is a shift towards a more ethical, socially-responsible approach, it's normally commercially driven. It'll be a long time before economics or public opinion brings about a change like this.

10. The amount of irrationality that executives attribute to others is directly proportional to their own.

Executives almost always consider themselves to be rational. But they tend to consider all those – subordinates, competitors, suppliers, customers – who disagree with them on any issue to be irrational. This *is* irrational.

For example, executives of a foundation that supported family planning efforts in developing countries considered the large number of children produced per family in these countries to be irrational. The fact is that few of these countries provided any form of social security; therefore one could only survive the unemployment that inevitably came with age if one had enough children to provide financial support. To try to convince those with no access to social security and insufficient income to provide it for themselves, to have fewer children is to ask them to commit a delayed suicide. Now who is irrational?

In an organization, problems created by the behavior of others cannot be solved by assuming them to be irrational. They can only be solved by assuming the others are rational, finding the point of view that makes them so, and addressing that rationally. The first detergent on the market failed despite its superior cleaning power. Attributing this to the irrationality of the housewife led nowhere. But assuming she was rational and trying to find its basis revealed that she estimated the cleaning power of a product by the amount of suds it produced. The original detergent produced none. *Tide* then came onto the market producing suds and success.

The problem isn't that irrational managers accuse others of being irrational, it's that they don't have the skills needed to listen to, and understand, other people's point of view. Had the soap powder executives found what the housewives really wanted they wouldn't have provided something that didn't hit the spot. It's a basic but common mistake. Managers either assume that others think the same way as they do or they're not really interested in finding out.

In sales or marketing it's really important to listen and to understand your customers' needs. If you don't, you're unlikely to get the business. I've been shocked that many sales people can't do this. They listen for just long enough to get what they think is a buying signal and start talking about their products. Real listening and the desire to understand are critically important for businesses. Lots don't realise it – few do it well.

Listening is different to hearing. Good communicators assume they don't necessarily know what people mean. For example, if a customer says he wants an easy-to-use mobile phone we have to find out what he means by easy-to-use; his definition may be very different from ours. If we do find out then we've listened and are much less likely to judge him to be irrational. We can also make the kind of phone he wants.

The best managers are genuinely interested in finding out what other people think and have superb listening skills.

11. The future is better dealt with using assumptions than forecasts.

Forecasts are about probabilities; assumptions are about possibilities. We carry a spare tire in our cars not because we forecast we will have a puncture on our next trip but because we assume a flat tire is possible. We plan for serious contingencies (floods, hurricanes, illness), however unlikely they may be.

Carrying a spare tire cannot prevent our having a flat tire but it can reduce its undesirable effect; for example, being stranded on a remote highway at night in the rain.

Of course there are futures that cannot be anticipated. These can't be planned for but they can best be met by flexible organizations, ones that can quickly detect the need to change, and are ready, willing and able to do so. For example, the driver of an automobile cannot predict all the conditions he or she will meet on the road but his or her ability to respond quickly and effectively removes the need to do so.

There is nothing that reduces the need to anticipate the future as much as the ability to respond rapidly and effectively to whatever it turns out to be.

The thermostat that controls the heating-cooling system in a building does not have to predict future weather in order to control it.

Yes. The key to dealing with the future is to be flexible and willing to learn. Those with most flexibility are the most adaptable. They have the skills to be able to do something different when what they are doing is not working or when they need to respond to changing circumstances. They are willing to accept that the future may turn out differently from how they anticipated and they relish that possibility instead of fighting against it. In the case of the rainy night turning into a night of flood, this might mean turning the spare tyre into a raft rather than using it to change the burst tyre! It might mean driving the car into a ditch in the case of a hurricane. Or it might mean driving on a flat if your passenger is seriously ill. Responding to changing circumstances is all about being creatively flexible – dextrous, in fact.

Those with a high need for control do not do well with changing futures. It makes them feel insecure and they hang on tightly to what they know while closing their eyes to the emerging reality around them. No good being in control of the thermostat if the oil has run out. The worrying thing is that most senior managers have a high need for control. They don't like to admit that they may have been wrong, that they may have made incorrect assumptions about the future. So the very people who are usually in charge of creating the futures of corporations are probably the least skilled to do the job.

12. An organization's planning horizon is the same as its CEO's retirement horizon.

The shorter the time to retirement of an organization's CEO the more it focuses on the short run and the less on the long run. In other words, an organization's planning horizon approaches zero along with the tenure of its CEO. It then takes a quantum leap when a successor comes on board.

Most executives care more about preserving their reputations after their retirement than about the preservation of the organizations from which they retire. If, subsequently, their previous organization suffers it can always be blamed on their successors. No executives want to bequeath to their successors the opportunity to take credit for what they have done. But they want their successors to take blame for any problems they may have passed on to them. Successors, on the other hand, want to attribute blame to their predecessors for any problems they cannot deal with effectively. Nowhere is this more apparent than in the presidency of the USA.

It is indeed rare for executives to care more about leaving a legacy than about building and preserving their own reputation.

CEOs who build great companies are the ones who leave the most successful and visible legacy. Unfortunately today the CEOs who come to our attention via the media are the types who are more in it for themselves.

The only hope is that the ambitions of the CEO coincide with what is good for the organisation so that there is a win/win. We can't blame CEOs entirely when they put their career first. The Board and shareholders are equally responsible. When things go well or badly these people are not held responsible, as they should be.

13. The lower the rank of managers, the more they know about fewer things. The higher the rank of managers, the less they know about many things.

Executives make mountains out of molehills; subordinates make molehills out of mountains.

The relationship between executives and subordinates is complementary: neither knows why the other does what they do, or cares about it. This leaves a large black hole between them into which most important issues and communications fall, lost and, like Clementine, gone forever.

The reason for this state of affairs is that executives are busy asserting their power and their staff are busy trying to impress. So much energy goes into the 'game'. Rarely do bosses and their staff stop and think 'what is our purpose here?' If they asked that question, answered it and acted on the answer then the black hole would disappear.

Why don't they do this? On the bosses' part, it's fear of losing control. On the subordinates' part, it's fear of getting it wrong.

The result: ineffectiveness and a stifling of creativity.

Antidote: focus on the questions: 'what are we trying to achieve?' and 'how can we support each other?'

Easier route: hire confident people (I mean truly confident people, not those who wear it as a mask to hide their insecurity) whose disposition is to be collaborative, who don't need to prove themselves and who are mature enough to say that they don't know, and so ask for help.

The best organisations provide the environment in which collaboration can flourish. Confident, competent people at all levels who share common goals relish collaboration and are open to filling in the 'gaps' in each others' knowledge.

14. The importance of executives is directly proportional to the size of their waiting rooms and the number of intervening secretaries.

Arrival at the executive's waiting room is only the first step in a fruitless process. Nothing is provided to keep one productively occupied while waiting. The higher the rank of the executive, the older and less attractive the intervening secretaries are. They form the Maginot Line that can only be breached by an armored vehicle. The secretary is one of those amazons who eventually notifies the caller that the sought-for executive has been called off on an emergency. He/she has escaped through a door not visible from the waiting room. It is not known when he or she will return.

Rain checks are not available because the executive's calendar is filled for the next month. With a smile on her face for the first time, the secretary advises, "Call again next month for an appointment."

Waiting rooms? I haven't been in a waiting room, except at the dentist's, since the 1980s.

This may be true of old-style professionals like some lawyers and accountants but today's executive office is more likely to have snazzy, designer sofas, glossy mags to read and wi-fi connection so that you can plug in your laptop while you're waiting. The glass walls that let you see what the person you are waiting to see is doing while she keeps you waiting echo the desire of the best organisations for transparency at a broader level.

The bottom line is that, with today's 'time-poor' (that means 'busy' in plain English) executive, if you're useful to her, you'll get in to see her.

Waiting rooms should provide not time-wasting spaces but great places in which to work whilst waiting to see a receptive executive.

15. When managers say something is obvious, it does not mean that it is unquestionable, but rather that they are unwilling to have it questioned.

The obvious may not be self-evident, not even evident to oneself. It is what one wishes everyone else would accept as evident without further discussion.

The more obviously true a belief is thought to be, the more reluctance there is to discuss it, and the less willingness there is to modify it in light of whatever discussion of it takes place. "Obvious" does not mean "apparent", but "resistant to doubt". Beware of the obvious; it is the antidote to curiosity – without which there is no creativity.

That which is apparently obvious is often wrong, but this is seldom obvious; for example, the once widely held belief that the earth is flat.

There are few mental exercises more intellectually rewarding than questioning the obvious. However, doing so can be dangerous physically, as Bruno and Galileo learned.

Indeed this is true. Beware anyone who says, 'it's obvious'. But understand why they are saying it.

There are actually two reasons why people might say that something is obvious. The first one is because to them it is apparent and so not open to doubt. They really believe it. But in that case, they should be held to account: they need to share the reasons behind their conviction.

The second reason, as the f-Law states, is more sinister: it's a word used by managers to stop others questioning them and to put others' views down too. It acts as a warning. It's a brave person that questions the 'obvious'. More questioning of the obvious is needed in life and work. Without questioning, progress cannot be made. Critique is what makes bad organisations good, and good organisations excellent.

16. The less sure managers are of their opinions, the more vigorously they defend them.

Managers do not waste their time defending beliefs they hold strongly – they just assert them. Nor do they bother to refute what they strongly believe is false. For example, they would not defend the statement, 'It is necessary for the company to make a profit'. Nor would they refute the statement, 'It is not necessary for the company to make a profit'. To most managers the former statement is obviously true and the latter obviously false, hence neither requires defense.

Managers consider it futile to argue with those who do not accept what they consider to be obvious. But if one of their opinions of which they are not certain is attacked, they leap to its defense; for example, "Downsizing is necessary for corporate survival". It follows from this that a heresy is punished severely only when it involves beliefs that cannot be proven to be either true or false. Religion harbors the largest number of such beliefs. This is why religions experience more heresy than any other social institution. Management handles heretics more humanely than religious institutions; it does not burn them; it fires them.

Intelligent and open critique is the unspoken subtext here and this follows on from the previous f-Law which referred to the need to question the obvious. Corporate heresy is a problem that flourishes within a rigid hierarchy. So, how would an effective critique process work?

In your second example, 'Downsizing is necessary for corporate survival', the good manager will always question an action that will have severe fallout for colleagues or that may not have clear and simple outcomes. He or she will actively seek alternative strategies, compare the financial and 'value' costs, and then build an argument to persuade others that the conventional wisdom isn't necessarily the right action for the organisation this time. Perhaps there's another way; one that maintains a loyal and talented community of co-workers, achieves cutbacks and efficiencies in other ways, or that makes additional use of their resource in other areas. If the manager thinks he or she is right, any challenges to the argument will be seen as an opportunity to test its strength.

Of course this type of manager in a hierarchical organisation is rare because it requires putting the ego and complacency to one side. This is tough. The need to be 'right' at all costs projects heresy onto critics. It loses you the best talent. And it blocks innovation.

17. The more lawyers an organization employs, the less innovation it tolerates.

An executive, who was not in jail at the time, once asked a retired professor of law why, whenever he asked his corporate lawyers whether he could do something new, they always said, "No". The professor replied that the executive deserved such an answer because he was asking a stupid question. The executive was shocked by this reply and said he did not understand. The ex-professor of law went on to explain. "A principal responsibility of your corporate lawyers is to keep you out of jail. You are out of jail when you ask if you can do something new. Whatever you are doing when you ask the question is apparently safe; therefore, no risk of jail is involved in no change. But doing anything differently could involve a risk, however small. Hence the lawyers' 'No'".

"Then what," asked the executive, "should I ask?" "Don't ask anything," the retired law professor said. "Tell them what you are going to do and remind them that it is their job to keep you out of jail when you do it." Permission is almost always harder to obtain than forgiveness.

It depends on the lawyers. Great ones will be first and foremost committed to and excited by the business. Then they will take it as their job to ensure that all the innovative things that the business wants to do can be done in a way that the business and the people in it are protected by the law. A great lawyer is creative. And I don't mean like 'creative' accountants!

It's the special ones that can handle both the left brain and right brain requirements of their job. The good ones are not just guardians of the rulebook but are also 'how can I make this possible?' types of people.

So much depends on what the lawyer is like. A few <u>do</u> exist that you can talk to, look at the possibilities with and know are committed to helping you get your end result. On the other hand there are the nay-sayers who regard it as their job to tell you the legal position. Full stop. The latter would surely prove to be a block to innovation. My advice to the CEO who wants innovation is to find someone else and <u>definitely</u> don't let the blockers do any hiring.

18. Good teachers produce skeptics who ask their own questions and find their own answers; management gurus produce only unquestioning disciples.

Gurus produce disciples who disseminate without modification the doctrines they provide. Therefore, they put an end to the felt need to learn more. No disciple ever knew more than the guru who indoctrinated him or her.

Good educators encourage others to develop ideas that are better than the ones they, the educators, present to them. Good educators produce students who know more than *they* do. They produce skeptics by focusing on unanswered questions and unsolved problems, and encourage them to seek answers and solutions. Educators hope to produce students who will lead, not follow.

Gurus do not educate, they indoctrinate. They provide answers, not questions or problems. They produce gospels and apostles, followers and believers, and often fanatics. Fanatics consider only a limited number of questions to be legitimate; these are the questions to which they believe they have been provided with correct answers. All other questions are considered to be unworthy of answering.

Management gurus peddle panaceas, simple solutions to complex problems. The only consultants more harmful are those who peddle complex solutions to simple problems.

Even more scary than this is that they are listened to more than the insiders who know the business far more than some management guru can.

Many companies spend millions on management gurus without ever thinking to impose performance measures on them in the way that they do on their own workers. Something about their status renders them unquestionable – I guess it's a quasi-religious thing.

Management gurus set themselves up as experts. <u>Still</u>. And in a world where experts are increasingly losing value as the age of the learning organisation approaches. How does that happen when clearly there is more value in those who help us to learn than in those who tell us the right answers? It's because our corporations and schools are pretty slow on the uptake.

19. The only thing more difficult than starting something new in an organization is stopping something old.

The momentum of an organizational practice is proportional to its age. Practices are harder to stop the older they are. Innovations have no age, hence no momentum, and therefore are easy to stop.

As Ambrose Bierce, the great American wit, noted, there is an infinite number of reasons for not doing something, but only one reason for doing it: it is the right thing to do. But this is very hard to prove.

This is why, for example, old generals do not die; they fade away slowly while serving as experts on television. Retired executives and generals become experts when they are freed of responsibility for their opinions. It is amazing how capable retired generals and executives become in solving the problems they could not solve before they retired.

Ah! This is actually all about <u>motivation</u> and momentum. If you want to do something – whether it's to start something or stop something – and you have the momentum, you can do it. It's as simple as that. With the right people and the right reasoning, innovations can certainly gain momentum and create change.

Older practices can be extremely easy to stop for the same reasons. An example would be Internet use for an older person. They are used to contacting their grandchildren by letter. Suddenly they find they get no correspondence back because the grandchildren are all using email. The motivation is there now. The grandparent just needs to be shown how to send an email (rather than reading up on it in books in the library in which case the momentum would likely be lost) and, hey presto, finds they get an instant reply from their beloved. The old practice – letter writing – stops very quickly.

20. Acceptance of a recommended solution to a problem depends more on the manager's trust of its source than on the content of the recommendation or the competence of its source.

One who receives a recommendation can never share the entire process that led up to it. It is always possible that there is an undetected aspect of the recommendation that could harm the recipient, even if unintentionally. For this reason, the more the recipient trusts the one making the recommendation, the more likely it is to be accepted.

No amount of competence can compensate for a lack of trust. Friendship is an ultimate act of trust; therefore, it is the advice of friends, however bad, not that of enemies, however good, that is most likely to be followed.

Friends are ones who can be trusted to make decisions in our best interest even when doing so involves sacrificing their own. A friend always tries to do what is perceived as best for us, which is something we do not do for ourselves.

It is much easier for an organization to protect itself against an enemy's conscious efforts to harm it than to protect itself against harmful acts done unconsciously by friends. Well-intentioned acts based on ignorance can do more harm than badly intentioned acts based on knowledge. Ignorance is a much more serious enemy than ill will.

Thank goodness trust still plays a huge part in our decision-making even in these days when organisations are obsessed by metrics, data and logic. In corporations we tend – or, perhaps more accurately, pretend – to treat the 'hard' evidence as all that counts. We deny the emotional reasons for our decisions. We're human beings: it follows that the baseline for most of our decisions is emotional, and that we justify our decisions using logical rationale retrospectively. This is because in a logic-based culture, it seems counter-intuitive to suggest that rational decisions are often grounded in emotion and gut feeling.

Whether it's acknowledged or not, trust is one of the most fundamental determinants of the health or an organisation. Thankfully that's not about to change anytime soon.

To say that well-intentioned acts based on ignorance can do more harm than badly-intentioned acts based on knowledge is not true at all. Both can be equally harmful. If someone is badly intentioned it's irrelevant whether or not they have knowledge. A bad intention can never not harm. What is more, a bad intention, by its nature, is disguised. This makes it even more insidious and dangerous. A good intention based on ignorance may be helpful by chance; a bad intention, by definition, can never be helpful.

21. The less managers understand their business, the more variables they require to explain it.

$E = mc^2$ (the special theory of relativity) contains only one independent variable, m, and explains what may well be the most complicated phenomena understood by scientists. Then why does it take thirty-five variables to understand why people select the retail store or the cereal they use? The answer is apparent: these phenomena are *not* understood. The less something is understood, the more variables are required to provide an alleged explanation of it.

Understanding provides managers with a way of determining the relevance of information. This is why managers who do not understand what is happening want all the information about it that they can get. Not knowing what information is relevant, they fear omitting anything that might be. Consequently, they suffer much more from an oversupply of irrelevant information than from a shortage of relevant information.

And what's more, they feel the need to create a huge amount of quantifiable evidence to back them up in case they make the wrong decision and get blamed for it.

We're back to insecure managers. There is no way that they will take risks, make decisions based on intuition or go with their gut. No, they need hard, scientific evidence. Even when it's clearly not scientific, as long as it has that appearance it's good enough.

22. The higher the rank of managers, the less is the distance between their offices and their restrooms.

Corollary 1: **The distance between offices is directly proportional to the difference between the ranks of their occupants.**

Corollary 2: **The higher a manager's rank, the less distance there is between his/her office and his/her parking space.**

The principal privilege enjoyed by those of high rank is minimization of the distances they must walk. Their restrooms are normally located adjacent to their offices or within them. For some executives their restrooms are their offices.

It is considered demeaning for one of high rank to walk to the office of a subordinate or to another floor of the headquarters building (other than the floor containing the executive dining room or barber). This all follows from the assumption that the length of executives' legs is inversely proportional to the circumference of their rank.

"Walk the talk" is futile advice to executives because for them walking and talking are incompatible activities. They can do only one at a time. Therefore, they choose to talk. It takes less effort and thought.

Some still have their own restrooms to save them having to bump into their subordinates in such a vulnerable space.

The same goes for the parking space – if they had to walk too far they might face all sorts of 'uncontrolled' encounters with staff.

The CEO at a company I used to work for, when he joined the company, got rid of allocated parking spaces. Those who got to work first got the best parking spaces. It was a symbol that privilege based on power was a thing of the past. It was a very clear signal and a simple but smart move.

This is the way the best organisations are going, although I imagine that at the very top of many companies such privileges and symbols of status will remain. That's a shame. And a mistake.

23. Business schools are as difficult to change as cemeteries, and for the same reasons.

Tenure anesthetizes the minds of most faculty members, as much as job security does to managers who enjoy it; it produces a complacency that encourages early retirement of minds. There is no better guarantee of security than increasing competence, and none that discourages such increases more than tenure.

In the first half of the twentieth century tenure was seldom granted to a faculty member before the age of fifty. Therefore, the decision to grant it was based on performance over twenty-five to thirty years, and an expectation of continued productivity over no more than the next ten to fifteen years. Today, tenure is usually granted in the early thirties. This means it is often based on a very few years of teaching and research, and is based on a projection of continued productivity over thirty to forty years. Little wonder that these projections are so frequently wrong.

There are better ways of protecting academic freedom than tenure, but no better way of protecting incompetence.

This view seems to be based on the assumption that the faculty members who get tenure are motivated only by the security of their tenure. That is like saying that people become complacent and don't try anymore to please their partner once they're married. Some do, some don't. Are there not tenured faculty members who are as committed, energetic and competent as they would have been had they not secured tenure because for them there is intrinsic motivation in the work they do?

Of course, that does not mean that the very notion of tenure isn't a strange and outdated one. The rationale for it is difficult to understand. Maybe it's one of those many organisational practices that survives for decade after decade without anyone questioning or challenging it.

24. Curiosity is the "open sesame" to learning, even for managers.

Preschoolers are curious about almost everything. Postschoolers are curious about almost nothing. They think they already know everything they need to know.

Schools, including business schools, restrict the kinds of questions that may be asked by students to ones that are not controversial and for which answers are thought to be available. Not permissible are such questions as: why, in the richest country in the world, are there more than forty million people living in poverty and a similar number who have no, or inadequate, health care coverage? Why does the United States have the second highest percentage of its population in prison of any country and simultaneously the highest crime rate? Of the many gods believed in around the world, which is the most authentic and who authenticates god? What is life and when does it begin?

Not only are children and managers taught not to ask the right questions, but they are also taught to provide expected answers, whether right or wrong, to the wrong ones. Advancement depends on it, in school and later in business. Creativity is killed in those restricted to asking expected questions and providing expected answers.

Effective leadership or management is not possible without creativity, but administration, which is frequently mistaken for both, *is* possible without creativity.

I couldn't agree more. We systematically knock the curiosity out of people starting at school age. The consequences of this are damaging both to the individual's development and also to organisations. Those who do manage to maintain their curiosity, who do ask the difficult questions and who do seek to understand genuinely, are seen as a bit of a pain. These are the people who rock the boat, and most organisations don't like them.

Most of us tend to go through our lives looking for evidence to confirm our beliefs. We don't go around trying to disprove ourselves. It makes us feel safe and secure to do this. Challenging ourselves and looking for where we may be wrong is something we don't do because it would disrupt our sense of ourselves and knock our confidence.

I was on an executive development course once where the trainer was working with a participant who was extremely attached to the way he had been doing things for years. It was clear to the rest of us that these ways were not that effective. I still remember the trainer's words that day: 'You would rather be right than happy'.

People or organisations spend a lot of time and energy proving to themselves that they're right about themselves. This attitude destroys any possibility of growth, development and change. All it does is guarantee the recycling of more of the same.

25. The legibility of a male manager's handwriting is in inverse proportion to his seniority.

She was just promoted

The less legible a male manager's signature is, the higher his rank and the more education he has had.

Female managers are genetically incapable of writing illegibly unless they are physicians. The illegibility of physicians' handwriting is the standard to which all other professionals, including managers, aspire. Illegibility of prescriptions prepared by doctors is responsible for the requirement imposed on pharmacists that they become psychics capable of reading the minds of physicians. The illegibility of handwritten memos from executives is similarly responsible for a similar requirement imposed on their secretaries.

Those managers who have not learned how to write illegibly can nevertheless accomplish the same thing by resorting to obscurity. Computers may help reduce illegibility but they have no effect on obscurity.

The illegible and obscure writings of managers hide what they know (if anything). The illegible and obscure writings of management educators hide what they don't know.

*Maybe we should use graphology more. The French swear by it.
That way there is no hiding place.*

*Otherwise, let's promote more women. We are generally much more
open, transparent, honest and happy to stand up and be counted.
Funny, but these are all characteristics of good leaders too. Men
(and bad leaders) spend too much energy on politics, spin, making
things look good, or trying to obscure things that are not favourable.*

*It's changing a little but men of my father's generation were brought
up believing that they had to be strong, know all the answers, not
show weaknesses and be better than other men. No wonder
businesses run by these characters are in such a state: when in
doubt, they blag it.*

*Legibility, rank and sex go together but if it's a man-thing, bring on
the women.*

26. Executives must be prevented from receiving any information about frauds or immoral acts committed by their subordinates.

This is referred to as the principle of blissful ignorance. The principle works both ways, symmetrically. Subordinates are not supposed to know about any illegal or immoral acts committed by their superiors.

In both cases this leaves very little for them to know.

The point here is the last line. In an unreconstructed organisation so much is kept in the shadows – motivations, intentions, desires (whether good or bad) and the essential humanity of its members.

Power, popularity, wealth, status are all motivators, whatever kind of organisation we work in. But in the best organisations employees at every level are free to admit and acknowledge their hopes and fears, what motivates them best and what drains their enthusiasm. It's a really difficult step to take and one that has to be taken first at the top. If the CEO can say 'I'm human' then everyone else can too. Employees at every level can then thrash out what's appropriate and acceptable and develop a culture and philosophy for the organisation that everyone can sign up to.

In the best organisations the stark reality is that illegal and immoral acts are visible. The principle of blissful ignorance is subsumed by shared knowledge and transparency.

27. There is nothing that a manager wants done that educated subordinates cannot undo.

The basis of this f-Law is as follows: the more "power-over" educated subordinates that managers exercise, the less is their "power-to" get them to do what they want them to.

"Power-over" is the ability to reward or punish subordinates for meeting or missing their boss's expectations. "Power-to" is the ability to induce them to do willingly what the boss wants them to. Therefore, the ultimate source of "power-over" is physical or economic, but the ultimate source of "power-to" is intelligence.

The effectiveness of "power-over" decreases as the educational level of subordinates increases. It becomes negative at the point when the educational level of the subordinates is higher than that of their bosses.

The exercise of authority is necessary for getting a job done by those who do not know how to do it, as, for example, in using aborigines to build a house. For those who know how to do it, the intervention of authority is an obstruction to getting it done, as, for example, in telling a plumber how to fix a leak.

'Power-to' also relies hugely on emotional investment. For followers to want to follow they have to feel some sort of emotional connection: loyalty, personal devotion to the vision, a genuine liking of the leader. Any or all of these will do.

It's hard to control any group of employees who are determined not to be controlled. Education sometimes plays a part but not always. However, I've seen many educated employees who have given in to authority for many different reasons. Education, of itself, does not equal the ability to resist unreasonable exertions of power nor the wherewithal to stand up for oneself or one's rights.

Subordinates who want to resist authority tend to do so in indirect and wily ways. Their ways of protesting tend also to be indirect. This is dangerous for bosses because it means that they may think that they are getting cooperation when actually their subordinates are passively resisting.

28. The more corporate executives believe in a free (unregulated) external market, the more they believe in a regulated internal market.

Internal service and supply units are seldom required to compete against external sources or each other for both internal and external business. If they were required to do so, this would prevent bloating, the creation of "make work", and eliminate a major source of the need for "rightsizing".

Unfortunately, managers who vigorously oppose the regulation of business by government, vigorously regulate the parts of their own businesses. Most enterprises operate with the same kind of centrally planned and controlled economy as was used in the Soviet Union. *Perestroika*, the replacement of a centrally controlled economy by a market economy, is as relevant to Western corporations as it was to the Soviet Union.

I think there's an Atlantic gap here. There's a growing resistance to 'market forces' and liberal economics on this side of the Atlantic. I want the state to intervene sometimes (to require more environmentally responsible behaviour by its citizens, for example), and I think the organisation's leadership needs to intervene and direct too, sometimes.

If departments have to compete internally as if it were a free market economy it may prevent 'bloating' but it also wastes time and resources. For me, collaboration and cooperation are the key to effective and efficient organisations. Internal competition doesn't help the company or its customers as the focus is on screwing the other guy not on doing the best possible job for the customer. Companies that have a strong culture of collaboration are able to tap into their resources fast and efficiently because people are predisposed to help.

Centrally controlled systems inhibit flexibility, responsiveness and innovation. Market systems can be responsive and flexible but only if the focus is on creating a win-win for the customer and supplier. Too much competition tends to create an obsession with beating competitors and results in the customer being neglected.

29. The amount of time a committee wastes is directly proportional to its size.

The amount of useful output generated by a committee decreases as its size increases. Therefore, the optimal size of a committee is zero or less. Committee meetings are a very efficient way of sharing ignorance and prejudices.

The function of committees is not to make decisions but to delay their being made long enough to allow the issue involved to fade away. A committee is an instrument for managing by default.

The value of a committee is judged to be proportional to the length of time and amount of money it requires to come to no conclusion, and the length of the report of the way it got there. The length of the report is inversely related to the amount of information it contains.

Those who convene committee meetings (or any meetings) should be required to pay for the time of those who attend. This would not only make meetings more productive but it would reduce their number and duration.

The word 'committee' is so loaded with negative connotations of bureaucracy and time wasting. If you slap on the label 'committee' you are probably unconsciously lowering everyone's expectations that they will achieve.

Any group of people that comes together to achieve a goal can do so in a vibrant and productive way or they can try hard in a drawn out and heavy way that yields little results. 'Committee' smacks of the latter so maybe we would do well getting rid of the term.

The nature of the working dynamic, the clarity of its goals and the motivation of its team members determine the effectiveness of a group more than its size.

A Management Committee Deliberating

30. It is generally easier to evaluate an organization from the outside-in than from the inside-out.

One of the principal reasons given by an organization for rejecting changes suggested by outsiders is their alleged lack of familiarity with the organization involved.

A change in the operations of a railroad was once suggested to an elderly railroad executive who then asked if the man proposing the change had ever worked on a railroad. He said no. The old man then asked if his father had ever worked on a railroad. Again he said no. The executive then asked if anyone in his family had ever worked on a railroad. The answer was still no. Then he asked why the one making the suggestion thought he was qualified to suggest how to operate a railroad. He replied by telling the executive a story that he had heard attributed to the architectural critic, Lewis Mumford. When Mumford was asked what right he had to criticize an architectural design, never having prepared one himself, he is alleged to have said, "I have never laid an egg but I know the difference between a good and a bad one".

The railroad executive was completely unfazed by this story. He said, "I was talking about railroads, not eggs". To say of some executives that they are dense is to say that their minds are very difficult to penetrate.

It's certainly much easier to see the organisation objectively when you look at it from the outside. But realistic internal observers can often see the subtleties and complexities of the culture in a way that outsiders can't. It's qualitatively very different to experience something and really 'feel' it and therefore understand what it's like than it is merely to observe it.

The man on the railway was right in that some knowledge of what it was like to work on the railway could certainly be useful. Not least in terms of the observer's empathy. By adding an intention to help, empathy improves the quality of our observations beyond what can be achieved with an intention simply to provide rigorous, impartial data.

The ideal evaluation team I would suggest is an external observer with excellent listening and observation skills and an internal observer with the felt experience of the system.

31. Development is less about how much an organization has than how much it can do with whatever it has.

How much an individual or organization has is largely a matter of wealth: how much has been earned or otherwise acquired. Standard of living is an index of wealth. How much one can do with whatever one has is a matter of competence: how much has been learned. It is reflected in the quality of life achieved.

The more developed individuals or organizations are, the less wealth they require to obtain a satisfactory quality of life. Equally, the more developed individuals or organizations are, the better the quality of life they can obtain with whatever wealth they have. A small, developed organization can provide a better quality of work life than a less developed one that is both richer and larger.

Robinson Crusoe is a much better model of development than J. Pierpont Morgan, Commodore Vanderbilt, or John D. Rockefeller. There are few organizations in which development is valued as much as, let alone more than, growth. A preoccupation with growth in an individual is pathological but it is generally considered to be healthy in organizations.

There is a multi-billion dollar industry geared towards helping individuals and organisations reach their true potential. It's a never-ending journey for those who choose to embark upon it. Some never start. Many don't even consider the possibility of the journey.

As for the growth/development debate, I doubt whether most leaders of corporations even think about these two concepts as distinct from each other. I doubt too whether they ever question their assumption that growth is good. Most would say, without question, that to grow is their purpose. Growth can easily be measured in hard quantitative terms. Development is much more difficult to define and measure so tends to be ignored.

32. Smart subordinates can make their managers look bad no matter how good they are, and make their managers look good no matter how bad they are.

The performance of managers depends more on their subordinates' performance than it does on their own, but their subordinates' performance depends little on that of their superiors.

A group of highly trained graduates often know more about their work than their bosses. In addition, they know that they know more, and that their bosses don't know this, and they break rules for which they know they can't be fired because their bosses' jobs depend on their performance. Hence, they may come to work in jeans, work odd hours, keep messy desks, and talk a lot to each other. This distracts their bosses but they know which side their butter is breaded on.

So a successful manager of highly educated subordinates is one who enables them to do whatever they want to do providing they also do the job the manager wants them to do.

So they think they're smart!

Actually, we're not talking about performance here; we're talking about the perception of their performance. Reputations are fragile. It only takes one or two negative stories about a person to ruin a reputation.

The aspects of actual performance that many organisations care most about are the financial ones. They will tolerate bad behaviour as long as someone is bringing in the numbers. They will not tolerate good behaviour if they are not achieving financial targets.

Subordinates can make their bosses' behaviour look bad more easily than they can make their results look bad. Badly behaved bosses don't usually care about that though. In fact some positively relish being perceived as hard-nosed and mean. Look at Donald Trump in the USA and Alan Sugar in the UK.

33. In an organization that disapproves of mistakes, but identifies only errors of commission, the best strategy for anyone who seeks job security is to do nothing.

This more than anything explains corporate resistance to change. Not changing threatens survival much more often than changing. In a turbulent environment it is usually better to do something than nothing. The only equilibrium that can be found when flying through a storm is dynamic.

The metaphor that is often invoked is to "keep your head down." Otherwise, obviously, it can be shot off. While individual managers may temporarily survive using this tactic, the organization's survival may be threatened by the failure to act in times of change.

An organization that always punishes mistakes risks meeting a future over which it has no control because managers were afraid to advocate changes that might avert future crises. A tolerance for mistakes can enable an organization to have a major role in creating its future.

One corporation distributed this statement to its managers: "If you didn't make a serious mistake last year, you didn't do your job; you didn't try something new. But if you make the same mistake next year, you won't be here the following year." In effect, this says that making a mistake is forgivable but only if learning results from it.

I agree. Disapproving of mistakes of commission explains much corporate resistance to change. It's that disapproval that often leads to errors of omission. People are less likely to repeat errors of commission but errors of omission are a symptom of the inability of executives to learn that change is essential to long-term survival.

We were taught in school that to please the teacher you needed to have the answers. Teachers know about the acquisition of knowledge, but too often they don't know about the learning process. Learning is a sophisticated skill. It requires self-knowledge, the ability to reflect, the willingness to change and a deep sense of self-confidence, which is needed to be able to stay in a state of uncertainty and 'conscious incompetence'.

Many worthy HR people struggle to rectify this by providing management training courses – but by then it's too late. In any case, the corporate culture subverts their valiant efforts.

Understanding the learning process and the culturally instilled inability to learn is probably one of the most serious crises facing modern corporations, if not our society as a whole.

34. The best organizational designers are ones who know how to beat any organization designed by others.

The better a system designer is at beating systems the more likely he or she is to design a system that is difficult to beat. Some systems are foolproof, but there are none that are proof against smart people. No one can design an organization that someone else cannot beat, especially if they have the help of lawyers. No lawyer ever wrote a law or regulation that precluded other lawyers from making a living out of beating it. For every organization there is a lawyer somewhere who can beat it by hook or crook, especially crook.

Contrary to popular belief, even government-imposed constraints and restrictions can be beaten, especially with the help of lobbyists who are lawyers in disguise.

A business-school course on "How to beat systems" would be the most valuable course a future manager could take. It is not offered because what would be learned in such a course could be turned against the school in which it was learned. There are few systems that are as worthy of being beaten.

I think it's more complicated – and more positive – than that. There is a two-tier system at work in most organisations. The best organisational designers are those who understand what's going to do the job. They also understand the importance of context; of designing something that is going to work in the particular system in which it sits. What is more, they understand the need for flexibility and constant redesign.

The best organisational designers are not ones who care about beating any system designed by others. The best care about creating something that is going to deliver the required results. Part of this process will be to make it workable by the people in whose system it sits. Another part will be to deter others from interfering with it. Of course, in a sense these people <u>are</u> beating the system by bypassing the lawyers altogether.

I have found that the best organisational designers are ones that have worked in the particular organisation, understand the culture, the pressures for and against change, and the people. What is more, they understand that often the formal design that is drawn on that piece of paper in the CEO's office bears no relation to the network that actually gets thing done in that particular organisation. The best organisational designers rarely carry the title. The best ones are the great leaders who understand how the system works and care passionately about wanting it to work better.

Sally Bibb – response

35. The offence taken by an organization from negative press is directly proportional to its truthfulness.

Nothing can offend an organization more than the truth about itself. It is easy for it to defend itself against lies but very difficult to do so against truths. This is why so many organizations would rather settle suits out of court; doing so conceals truths. The rationalizations given seldom reflect this fact.

What organizations seek from others, including the press, is reinforcement of the delusions they have about themselves. They never see themselves as others do, nor do they see others as they do. The result is an equitable distribution of distortion.

In this respect, organisations are no different from people. We all know people who don't like to hear the truth about themselves (though this law never applies to ourselves, of course).

But more frightening than the fact that organisations get it wrong sometimes is the fact that they are allowed to settle out of court. In many cases, doing this is effectively an admission of guilt, but as you say, often they're not held to account for it.

However, if it's reported, settling out of court exposes the fact that the company has done something wrong and is being made to pay. And that is, I suppose, one way of being called to account. But it doesn't go to the level that it should do which is to make sure that the offence cannot be committed again. At worst it's a way of paying people off. That's why the PR industry is so big and why people trust organisations so little.

36. The less important an issue is, the more time managers spend discussing it.

More time is spent on small talk than is spent on large talk. Most talk is about what matters least. What matters least is what most of us know most about. The more something matters, the less we know about it.

Everyone is an expert on trivia. So everyone can discuss trivialities with equal authority and at great length. This is not true with important issues on which there are alleged experts. Experts, those who know a great deal about a subject, tend to limit discussion to what they know about it. Their authority is vulnerable to new ideas, which, of course, seldom come from other experts, but from non-experts whom experts try to exclude from the discussion.

Experts seldom accept any responsibility for errors resulting from following their advice. However, they accept full responsibility for any successes that result from following their advice, however remote the connection.

This is a serious malaise. Managers feel comfortable discussing trivial issues because there's less at stake. Important issues cause trouble because discussions about them can lead to people taking difficult decisions. Difficult issues don't usually need experts to solve them. They need willing people to try to understand, evaluate, make a decision and then do something. This is risky.

The more difficult the issue the more likely it is that there isn't one right answer. Managers prefer it when there is only one right answer because it lessens the risk of making a mistake. Difficult issues are often also problems whose solution is a journey not a destination. You can start solving the problem only to find that it's not working out as you wanted. Then you need to change course. Many managers would rather die than change course. Sometimes there can be overwhelming evidence that the original decision wasn't the best one and that something else needs doing. Some managers see that as having to admit that they were wrong, which they were. They see something wrong in admitting they were wrong. In fact, it's a valuable thing to do.

In the best organisations, people have no qualms about changing course or admitting mistakes. Their aim is to resolve an issue. When Edison invented the light bulb it took thousands of attempts. He saw each one as increasing his understanding of what didn't work. He didn't see them as failures.

37. The time spent waiting to get into an executive's office is directly proportional to the difference in rank between the executive and the one waiting to get in.

A caller of higher rank than the executive is shown in at once even if it means waking him up.

Alcoholic beverages are offered to those of higher rank when they enter. Coffee is offered to those of the same rank as the executive whose office it is. Nothing is offered to those of lower rank. Those of the lowest rank are not seated.

Rank has its privileges

It's certainly true that those more powerful have the licence to keep those less powerful waiting and the latter of course won't complain. They know their place.

It's surprising to me how many people don't offer a drink of any kind to a visitor. And how many visitors are surprised when you offer them one. Surely this is common courtesy and good hospitality?

As for being offered alcohol, that surely is a thing of the past in most companies. And those of lowest rank not being seated? Those dinosaurs who would make us stand do still exist in some dark, murky corners of the corporate world, hopefully with not long to go to extinction.

'Evolved' executives will know the value of what's being said to them without reference to rank or title. A sense of reciprocal responsibility engenders trust and shared priorities.

38. Administration, management and leadership are not the same thing.

Administration is the direction of others in the pursuit of ends and by the use of means both selected by others.

Management is the direction of others in the pursuit of ends and by the use of means selected by a manager.

Leadership is the direction of others in the pursuit of ends and by the use of means that they collectively select.

Those who follow a leader do so voluntarily. He/she takes them where they want to go. Leaders do not exercise authority over followers; managers do. Those who command and control do not lead; they manage.

Administration is the controlling of others in the pursuit of ends and by the use of means both dictated by others.

Management is the directing of others in the pursuit of ends and by the use of means decided by others.

Leadership is the inspiring of others in the pursuit of ends and by the use of means that they collaboratively select, and that they are flexible enough to change as the environment changes.

Those who follow a leader do so enthusiastically and willingly. It's a 'towards' mentality: going towards what you believe in. It's leaders using Russ and Herb's 'power-to' (see f-Law 27).

Those who follow a manager do so because they are worried about the consequences of not doing so. It's an 'away from' mentality: avoiding what you don't want to happen, i.e. being disciplined or fired.

39. In acquisitions the value added to the acquired company is much more important than the value added to the acquiring company.

The price required to acquire a company is almost always greater than it is currently worth. Therefore, it is important for the potential acquirer to estimate how much value it can add to the acquired company. How much would the acquired company be worth taking this added value into account?

The reason that most acquisitions do not turn out to be successful is that the value of the acquired company decreases after the acquisition. This, in turn, reduces the value of the acquiring company.

Due diligence at best reveals the current value of an acquisition candidate. Diligent planning of how to enhance its value is required. Such planning is the most diligent thing a potential acquirer can do.

Senior executives in acquiring companies would probably agree with this. But they don't act as though they do. They acquire companies for all sorts of reasons – of course all the reasons are to do with ultimately increasing their own value. When they have acquired a company they tend to work hard at every turn to squeeze the last drop of benefit out of it.

With ownership comes power. The usually unspoken attitude is to wield power to make sure that the acquired company knows who's in charge. The acquired company has to yield to the demands of the new owner to make them more efficient, effective, change their ways, change their culture, etc. Which is something it always resists. And for the acquirer, it's is all about being able to prove to the shareholders and investors that the right decision was made. When that kind of pressure is on, a command and control style tends to kick in rather than a collaborative style.

Despite the huge number of acquisitions that have been made, the lessons don't seem to be learned. No corporation stands out as being really good at it. The master/servant relationship gets in the way time and time again.

40. Business schools are high security prisons of the mind.

Business schools restrict or deny freedom of choice. They specify what must be taught, and when and how. What is scheduled is teaching, not learning.

Under the pretext of evaluating students, business schools prohibit "cheating" by making minds work in solitary confinement. When taking examinations or preparing work, collaboration is a no-no. But once students enter the *real* world, what was taken to be cheating in school becomes highly valued collaboration with others in the quest for understanding. Business schools discourage learning from others even though it is the principal way those who graduate learn for the rest of their lives.

Managers are not evaluated by what they can accomplish without help but by what they can accomplish with all the help they can get. How to use others effectively is one of the most important things a manager can learn, but it is a dangerous thing to try to learn in a business school.

Faculty members do not motivate students to continue learning after leaving school. They remove the perceived need for further learning by pretending to provide all the answers students will ever need. Their perception of what students will need after graduation is rarely tainted by any contact with reality.

True, but who are the customers? The students. But the students' employers are customers too as it's usually they that pay the bills. They can determine what they buy. So they must be held equally responsible for the methods used by business schools.

Learning from others is key. It's one of our prime methods of life-long learning. We get no formal practice in it. Ancient societies recognise and ritualise this kind of learning. In modern society we haven't got the knack, nor do we place enough value on learning from others.

It's broadly the same for academic learning. Collaboration is never encouraged. I have only ever heard of one Masters Degree (I did it) based on peer learning and evaluation. The learning was the best I have ever done. Why? Because it was collaborative – we were expected to learn from each other and to help one another to learn. Also from ourselves by doing a rare thing among executives – reflective learning. We were held accountable for our own and others' learning or lack of it. If someone wasn't good enough we failed them and then supported them to meet the required standards. We truly learned skills of learning and collaboration. Organisations could be transformed if they had those skills.

The biggest irony is that business schools – those revered seats of learning – run programmes on management and organisational development. They know the theory better than anyone, but they don't practice what they preach.

41. No matter how large and successful an organization is, if it fails to adapt to change, then, like a dinosaur, it will become extinct.

To determine how an organization would destroy itself by not adapting to change requires determining the future "it is now in". This is the future it would have if it were to continue its current behavior and the environment were to change only as expected. The future based on these assumptions, both false, is then projected out to the organization's inevitable self-destruction.

Self-destruction is inevitable on this basis because the organization would not adapt to even expected changes in its environment. The point is to reveal the Achilles heel of the organization, the source of its potential self-destruction. It also suggests how such self-destruction can be avoided.

In the 1970s such a projection revealed that, should the Federal Reserve Bank continue to clear checks in the same way, the number of check clearers eventually required would exceed the US population. Such a situation will obviously be avoided. But it could be avoided by either what is done to the bank or what the bank does. By FRB taking the initiative, it created its own future. It initiated development of the electronic fund transfer system, which reduced the rate of increase in the number of checks per year and eventually their absolute number.

In the case of the FRB it successfully created a new future with new possibilities for banking. Retrospectively it's easy to see how important that first electronic step was. Since the advent of the Internet this is fast becoming the way of business. Not only is the Internet age forcing more traditional businesses to think and act differently but, as excitingly, a new generation of workers is doing the same.

Large corporations tend still to have hierarchical structures and a command and control style of managing. But the world is changing. People want different things from work. There is a different model of organisation emerging. The cultures in these organisations are founded on trust. They hire good people, make clear agreements about what they are going to do and deliver and then let them get on with it. These are creative places to work that encourage innovation. They are not necessarily new Internet-age companies either. WL Gore and South West Airlines have both been around a long time.

Corporations that don't notice this or don't see it as a threat had better watch out. People increasingly want meaning from their work. Good people will vote with their feet and go to work for organisations that offer stimulating and supportive environments. With this in mind it's certainly feasible to imagine that big, traditional organisations could easily become extinct.

42. The size of a CEO's bonus is directly proportional to how much more the company would have lost had it not been for him or her.

Corollary: The size of a CEO's bonus is also directly proportional to (a) the number of people he/she has laid off, and (b) his/her responsibility for the apparent need to do so.

A company's increase in stock price after downsizing is proportional to the number of people laid off, providing none of them are executives. As most executives have learned, they can increase their bonus further by leaving the company after selling it or having assured its demise.

The demise of a company is always attributed to external – never internal – conditions it could not control. The national economy is always available to be blamed, as is unfair (and possibly illegal) competition. Mistakes that can't be accounted for in this way can be attributed to the irrational behavior of employees (especially if unionized), suppliers or customers.

One of the wonderful things about publicly listed companies is that we get to know exactly how much money senior executives are paid to 'go away'. Messing up is certainly financially advantageous if you're at the top of the tree and are given a big pay-off. Not so, further down. When you get fired for not performing your career prospects are seriously inhibited afterwards. CEOs who walk away with a golden handshake often don't work again afterwards because they don't need to. Otherwise they go into consultancy and manage to play on other CEOs' misguided assumptions that, as they've run a company, they must know what they're talking about.

Years of public outrage at the disproportionate scales of top executives' remuneration, when unjustified, have changed very little. As with the fight against corruption, it's only when the right-thinking of autonomous employees combines with a real shift in public values that things can begin to happen differently.

43. The less managers expect of their subordinates, the less they get.

Most of our expectations of others and ourselves are self-fulfilling prophecies. For example, teachers learn early that if they expect students to cheat, their students will not disappoint them. They will go to extremes to meet their teachers' expectations.

Children try hard to meet their parents' expectations no matter how unreasonable they are. The same is true of subordinates of managers. Managers try to lower what their superiors expect of them in order to appear to be performing above expectations. The result: lower expectations and lower performance.

This is true for those subordinates who are externally referenced to their manager. In the best organisations, more people are internally referenced, i.e. they decide what to expect of themselves and they judge whether they are doing a good job.

Many capable people, even in evolving organisations, have bosses who are inadequate in some way. These people can and do operate to their own standards despite what their boss says. For these people it's more about what they expect of themselves not what the boss or anyone else expects of them.

44. The amount of money spent to broadcast a television or radio commercial is inversely related to its truthfulness and relevance.

There should be a law that enables class action suits to be filed against advertisers who make false or misleading claims. There isn't such a law because elimination of such claims would put most media out of business. Furthermore, there are not enough courts and judges to handle the caseload that would result, but there are enough lawyers. Suing false claimers would provide lawyers with something socially useful to do. No wonder they do not do it!

The only commercials that avoid misleading the viewers or listeners are those that leave them wondering what product or service is being advertised. However, even bad television commercials provide intermissions that can be useful biologically. How much better such breaks would be if only the benefactor was identified and not his or her product or service. The absence of truth in TV advertising is not nearly as important as its lack of relevance.

For sure it can be a very fine line between spin and selling. There are those who make false claims and there are those who are just very good at portraying their products in an extremely compelling way. There is nothing wrong with the latter.

I am not so concerned about this because in the end it's the consumer who decides. Consumers these days are far more savvy and have far more power than they used to because they have a lot more choice. There is also a lot of consumer information on the Internet. The Internet provides them with the ability to tell a lot of people if others have been duped by false claims about a product or service. Consumers quickly see through illusions and can now literally tell the world online.

The cleverer the marketers become, the more the Internet comes into its own as a regulator of their activities. It's one area where technology and people power has really come together. The best companies know the importance of customer power and reflect this in their approach to advertising.

45. All work and no play is a prescription for low quantity and quality of outputs.

In the Renaissance, human activities were dissected into four categories: work, play, learning, and inspiration. The West then developed institutions where each of these could be engaged in to the exclusion of the others. Factories and business offices, for example, are designed for work, not for learning, fun, or inspiration. Country clubs are designed to provide fun, not work, learning, or inspiration. Museums and churches provide learning and inspiration but neither of the other two. Schools provide learning, but none of the other three.

The effectiveness of an activity and the joy that can be derived from it depends on the extent to which all four of these aspects of life are integrated. Therefore, ideal corporations, country clubs, schools, and museums would be distinguishable from each other only by their emphasis. A few such corporations exist; very few.

Oh, *how right you are. Those organisations that understand that work, play, learning and inspiration are the four ingredients of excellence are the ones that will be successful above all others. There are indeed very few. Despite what we know about human performance we still ignore this. It's too complex for most organisations to get to grips with. Yet it's very simple. If you look at the level of the individual you can see how simple. Look at what a brilliant teacher does. He inspires his students to want to learn, he pushes them, challenges them and makes them work hard and he makes it fun. Human beings thrive on that.*

Organisations today rely on innovation in order to thrive and survive. Innovation cannot happen without creativity. Creativity can only occur if people are encouraged to break the rules, challenge, have fun and look at things in new and interesting ways. In today's organisation the ability to play is a rare and valuable asset. No longer should it be the preserve of the wild and wacky innovation companies.

46. A bureaucrat is one who has the power to say "no" but none to say "yes".

Bureaucrats can find an infinite number of reasons for rejecting any proposed change, but can find none for accepting it. Since they cannot say "yes", if they want to have a proposal accepted, they must pass it on to someone of higher rank. But to do this is to acknowledge a limit to their importance and, therefore, to lose face. Their self-esteem is directly proportional to the number of times they say "no", and inversely proportional to the number of times they say "yes".

In a bureaucracy a "no" cannot lead to what is considered to be an error, only a "yes" can do that. Therefore, within a bureaucracy, doing as little as possible is the best strategy for avoiding detectable errors.

Maybe it also gives them more of a feeling of power to stop something happening than to allow it. There are two pressures being exerted here. One is external – the bureaucracy within which they work. The expectation of a bureaucracy is that people will toe the line and follow the rules. The second is internal. It may be insecurity that causes them to want to wield power over others; it may be that they don't feel confident taking the risks involved in giving permission for something that those above them may not approve of. Each of these factors feeds the other and reinforces the unproductive nature of a bureaucracy. The best organisations aim to remove the expectation of compliance <u>and</u> eliminate the fear of getting things wrong.

There are obvious bureaucracies – in Britain some Civil Service organisations breed rule-followers. But this type of organisation is what it is and there is an honesty and acceptance about what it is and the limitations that come from that. What's more, everyone knows that Civil Service organisations are bureaucratic – even the people who work in them.

The really worrying organisation is one that thinks it's something else – the bureaucracy in disguise. There are entire organisations that fit this description and others where parts of them are run as stifling bureaucratic systems. These organisations with a deluded sense of what they are, really <u>are</u> in danger. Because without this recognition they will never be able to change the parts that are holding them back.

47. Teleconferencing is an electronic way of wasting more time than is saved in travel.

When one's attendance at a meeting is electronic, one cannot feel as much a part of it as when one is present. It is psychologically uncomfortable because body language is one of the most important forms of communication. This tends to make the meetings less participative and productive than those held in a conference room.

Unfortunately, the ease with which teleconferences can be set up is an incentive to hold more of them than are actually needed. Such meetings are also interpreted as evidence that an organization is "with" new technology.

The majority of communication between people is non-verbal. Body language, tone of voice, subtle facial changes – all of these transmit more than the words. Teleconferencing is therefore a very inadequate means of communication. What's more, people in the room tend to focus on the people who are not in the room so equal attention is not given to all participants. Perhaps that's because it takes more concentration to listen to the people whose contribution is transmitted via the screen or voice box.

Some companies are using teleconferencing more and more as a way of saving money and travel time. It's a false economy. For all but extremely transactional exchanges, teleconferences are inadequate. Techies may not understand that good communication always has depended on understanding and rapport. Electronic means of communication such as telephone, email and teleconferencing are about efficiency of communication. However, they actually hinder effective (i.e. affective) communication. Humans will always be humans and even the most rational of us respond emotionally to any given situation. We can't _not_ do this as humans.

Good communication is about responding emotionally to the stimulus from the other person. Corporations seem to spend a lot of time putting in place systems and procedures that ignore our human-ness.

48. The more important the problem a manager asks consultants for help on, the less useful and more costly their solutions are likely to be.

Consultants begin their engagements by gathering very large amounts of data, much more than can be transformed into useful information. No wonder! Their fees are proportional to the amount of time they devote to a problem, not to the amount of good that they do.

The most successful consultants are the ones who are smart enough to see what managers want and give it to them after an extended effort, and do so in long, impressively formatted reports. They provide sanctions for a fee.

The principal finding obtained by all studies conducted by consultants, regardless of the issues involved, is the need for more study. The success of a consultant's effort is not measured by the amount of good it does for the client, but the amount of good it does for the consultant.

It's astonishing that, in these days of obsession with return on investment, consultants are not held to account more than they are. There are three reasons for this:

1. Executives are seduced by data – the more they have, even if it's useless, the more it makes them feel in control.
2. The CEO or someone else very senior usually hires the expensive consultants. Who is going to challenge the CEO's decision?
3. Consultants set themselves up as experts. This provides the executive with another hiding place. 'If the expert says so who am I to disagree?'

Consultants – unlike the rest of us – do indeed manage to escape being accountable. The higher their fee, the less accountable they become. The more complex and costly their solutions, the more unlikely it is that they'll be challenged.

Who's going to want to point out that some senior executive's decision to hire consultants has been a huge waste of money?

The best organisations, by the way, are more likely to use internal consultants, form employee problem-solving teams or hire customers and suppliers to solve problems for them.

49. The distance between managers' offices is directly proportional to the difference between the ranks of their occupants.

Executives of the same rank have unconnected offices next to each other. This enables their secretaries to control access to their bosses, even by their peers. Their superiors do not come to their offices; they go to those of their superiors.

Subordinates who call are prioritized and stored in the waiting room for future reference.

Yes, in a bad organisation. Also the higher up they are in the building the higher their rank. Some executive floors are like those suites in 5 star hotels that are reserved for the rich and famous. You only get in there with permission and if you have some very important business to do or service to provide.

The superiors do not go to their subordinates' office? Oh so true. You're expected to go to them. When they are seen out and about it usually means trouble.

In the best organisations, the boss is one of the people. But beware bosses who are <u>trying</u> to be one of the people. They may actually visit the offices of those lower down than them and even talk to employees at their desks whilst on 'walkabout'. But usually this is all set up in advance. It's a contrivance. They have a 'guide' (a.k.a. bouncer) in case some disgruntled employee gets out of hand. Usually several days' notice is given so that the place can be tidied up in advance.

50. The *sine qua non* of leadership is talent, and talent cannot be taught.

One can be taught to draw but one cannot be taught to be an artist. The difference is talent, a gift at birth. One's talent can be enhanced. Tools and techniques can be transmitted to artists as well as to draftsmen. The essential requirement of a leader is an ability to inspire. Inspiration is an art, not a science. Leadership, then, is more an art than a science.

Leadership development courses and programs can develop those who already have the requisite talent but they cannot make leaders out of those who are without it. What such courses and programs do and do very well is make managers who cannot lead think they can.

The Leader & His Followers.

Many organisations are in denial about leadership. Most should probably ditch the term 'leadership' and resign themselves to the fact that what is going on is actually just management. Leadership is so rarely seen that it's impossible for most people to know what good leaders are.

Nelson Mandela is a fine example of a leader. His utter genuineness and vision inspires. He speaks from his heart, is strong and knows what he wants to achieve. He also listens and hears the views of others. This shows humility. The barging kind of person often heralded in American business is not a leader. True leadership is authentic. Leaders are worthy of our trust.

The common view of leadership has been warped by celebrity CEO images of someone who seems confident and charismatic but is actually putting on an act. Therein lies the problem with leadership courses. They teach people to act. Most of us can detect 'acting' and so we refuse to buy into it. When someone is passionately pursuing a cause, it inspires us, even when we don't fully share in it. We rarely see people like Mandela in business, perhaps because it's hard to be as passionately dedicated to business. Business is not a cause but a means of growing wealth. At a deep human level, that doesn't inspire.

What true leaders need is help to manifest their natural talents. Many a leader is a quiet, introverted type. Mandela himself is that way. But he has learned how to let his power shine through.

51. Managers who don't know how to measure what they want settle for wanting what they can measure.

For example, those who want a high quality of work life but don't know how to measure it, often settle for wanting a high standard of living because they *can* measure it. The tragedy is that they come to believe that quality of life and standard of living are the same thing. The fact is that further increases to an already high standard of living often reduce quality of life.

Unfortunately and similarly, the (unmeasurable) quality of products or services is taken to be proportional to their (measurable) price. The price of a product or service, however, is usually proportional to the cost of producing it, not to its quality; and this cost tends to be proportional to the relative incompetence of the organization that produces it.

Like economists, managers place no value on work they do not pay for because they can't measure it. Work that has no quantifiable output includes some of the most important work that is done, for example, raising children and maintaining a home. On the other hand, economists place a high value on work that destroys value, because the cost of such work can be measured. Hence the paradox: a prolonged war is a very good way of raising gross national product but also of reducing quality of life.

When it comes to life goals it's even more basic than that. Managers don't know what they want because they never think about it. One executive told his psychotherapist he was depressed because he felt he wasn't successful. To the therapist he looked successful: good job, great salary, lovely family and beautiful home. She asked how he would know when he was successful. He couldn't answer. He just kept on striving without knowing what he was striving for.

But I agree that, if they get as far as measuring, the measurement is usually quantitative and limited to how much they earn. Certainly the more they earn and the more their standard of living rises the more their quality of life drops. They become trapped by golden handcuffs.

In the workplace it's also true that managers will measure anything that can be quantified in order to be able to set targets. Training is a great example. Many companies measure numbers of days training and numbers of people trained. If the goal is to do lots of training then that's a good measurement. But the goal ought to be to develop the workforce to become more skilled. The best organisations explicitly develop employees to fulfil their potential and even advise them on finding jobs outside the organisation, if that's what it takes. Measuring skills is harder. It takes time and commitment and, often, the value of training cannot be quantified. How astonishing that such 'input' measures continue to be accepted as valid even though they are value-less.

52. A great big happy family requires more loyalty than competence, but a great big happy business requires more competence than loyalty.

Loyalty is much more important for the preservation of a family than for the preservation of a business. Allocating authority and responsibility in a family business on the basis of competence may well destroy the family but preserve the business.

In a family the weakest members usually receive the most care, attention, and resources. When carried over to a business this is a recipe for failure.

It is often better to pay a member of the family to stay away from the business than for becoming a part of it.

It does not have to be, and indeed should not be, either/or. Both are needed for any business to thrive. A family business potentially contains more emotional complexities than an ordinary business but it needs the same ingredients to run it.

Hiring for attitude (including loyalty) and training for skills (a.k.a. competence) is the way to go because the former is harder to get than the latter. Any business whose employees are loyal has a valuable asset. When loyalty is absent people are less committed. This is a problem for business whether it's a family business or not. It's just that disloyal family members can harm more than just the business. That is the issue.

53. If an organization must grow, it is better for it to grow horizontally than vertically.

Horizontal growth of organizations widens management's spans of control but retains the same number of layers. The more layers there are, the more difficult it is to integrate vertical interactions. The wider the spans of control, the easier it is to coordinate horizontal interactions.

The spans of control of managers in the US are generally much too narrow. This results in an excess of managers. The excess derives from the fact that in order to increase deserving employees' salaries beyond the maximum allowable for those of their rank, they must be promoted to a managerial position for which there is no need. If salaries were based on performance, not on rank or category, the surplus of managers would be reduced, spans of control widened, and layers decreased. Performance would increase.

American corporations – unlike most of their executives – have a profile like an hourglass: large spans of control at the top and bottom, and small spans in the middle.

The greater the excess of managers in the middle, the harder it is for the top and bottom to communicate with each other.

If it's a straight choice between an organisation growing horizontally or vertically then I agree that horizontal is better. But productive growth is achieved when the right people can work together effectively and efficiently and when they get the support of senior management. Span of control is less relevant. What matters is whether the manager can bring something to the group that he is leading. Most managers focus on monitoring and controlling their staff's actions. If it's just a matter of monitoring employees' activities then it doesn't matter whether spans of control are large or small. But if a manager is a leader and brings something in terms of vision, expertise, coaching and direction to the team then he is worth having around.

A horizontal structure lends itself to a networking style of working as opposed to a hierarchical structure, which leads to rigid control and inflexibility. Networks, provided that they have clear goals and the necessary mix of skills, are the most efficient ways of working.

Corporations run as hierarchies also have informal networks. They may not recognise them but they need them to make sure the right people connect with each other to get the job done. Of course they need to go through the 'official' channels as well, but the effective people in any organisation know who to engage and how to do that in order to get things done. That, together with vision and goals, is the way that organisations grow.

54. Corporate development and corporate growth are not the same thing and neither requires the other.

Cemeteries and rubbish heaps grow but do not develop; Einstein continued to develop without growing; in fact, he contracted as he aged. This is true of corporations too: they can grow without developing and develop without growing.

Growth is an increase in size or number. Development is an increase in competence, one's ability to satisfy one's own needs and legitimate desires, and those of others. A legitimate desire is one the satisfaction of which does not decrease anyone else's ability or desire to satisfy their own needs and legitimate desires.

Corpulence is a product of growth; competence a product of development. Growth is quantitative; development is qualitative. Growth is a matter of earning; development is a matter of learning. The objective of growth is to increase standard of living; the objective of development is to increase quality of life.

A corporation develops to the extent that it increases its ability to contribute to the development of its stakeholders. Growth may inhibit development but development cannot inhibit growth. Bigger is not necessarily better. The best reason a corporation can have for growing is to maintain or increase employment while increasing the productivity of labor. Here growth is a means, not an end.

If only corporations understood this. If they did, they would also hire people who are able to learn. The development of corporations can't happen unless the people in them know how to create change as opposed to just repeating what they already know over and over. It's those who can create change that develop personally and help their companies to grow.

Learning is an ability that we use when we are babies. At that age we are constantly trying new ways of doing things in order to be able to master important skills like walking and talking. As we get older and we learn more, we go to school and there we are taught to acquire knowledge. We are rewarded for having the right answer. We are not rewarded for trial and error – the very skills that we applied so well as infants and enabled us to learn quickly. The skills of learning are never explicitly taught or understood. This is fundamental and is a major gap in organisations today. And it seriously inhibits their ability to develop.

55. The uniqueness of an organization lies more in what it hides than what it exposes.

Public relations and corporate advertising are designed to create an illusion, a shadow that will be perceived by others as substantial. It is a product of wishful thinking. Just as the uniqueness of a person does not lie in the clothes he/she wears, the uniqueness of an organization does not lie in the words with which it dresses itself. It lies in what it does, not what it says about it.

One can differ without being unique, especially when many others differ in the same way.

It is much easier for an organization to create a unique logo and slogan than a unique work environment or even a unique product or service. Uniqueness is seldom the result of a deliberate and conscious act. It derives from the way and content of how an organization thinks and acts. Originality is not a commodity. It cannot be acquired from others; it must be developed from within.

I agree that originality is definitely not a commodity, it most certainly comes from within.

Originality cannot be acquired or developed. To have any hope of being unique you have to have your own genuine beliefs, values and passion. Organisations and people who try to be original usually fail miserably at it. Or they come across as fake, because they are. True originality comes from passion for something. Do the thing you believe in because you really want to; do it in an authentic way, and you stand a chance of doing something unique. Originality is a consequence not a goal; that's why it can be hard to spot, either from the inside or from without.

56. The telephone, which once facilitated communication, now increasingly obstructs it.

The telephone is now used to enable a synthetic source of speech to indicate to callers that those with whom they wish to communicate do not want to be reached. But it does give callers an opportunity to exercise their index fingers by pushing buttons before they are put on hold and subsequently cut off.

It once took only seven digits and a small amount of time to reach most people. Now the number of digits and the amount of time required have increased exponentially and exceed the capacity of a normal person's memory or patience.

The routing choices offered synthetically seldom reveal the choice one wants. This often leads to a vain effort to reach a person. In the rare case in which a person is reached, that person is unqualified to respond to the need of the caller and doesn't know who is. This initiates a series of transfers that terminates in a carefully programmed accidental cut-off.

The telephone, which once significantly reduced the need to write, is now driving us back to it.

A significant and growing barrier to communication is the automated response system. Where it once took only a couple of minutes to order cinema tickets on the phone it now takes way longer, more concentration on the part of the buyer (lose it for a minute and you have to start again) and no opportunity to ask non-standard questions. So in this you're right. The human touch is missing. This is a serious problem for companies that want to provide a good service.

More generally our rising expectations are the problem – not the phone. We now expect to be able to contact people more easily than before because of mobile communication and email. We can leave messages day or night. They can pick up these messages whether they are at work, home, on the move or on holiday. It's so easy to be communicated with that we increasingly want to be left alone, to at least have some choice about when we respond.

There is so much technology that can facilitate communication. But it cannot do that without the user making some choices about how easy he wants the communication to be. And making those choices does require new skills and strategies. The answer never lies in technology. Some businesses think it does and they are the ones who will lose out to the ones who realise that the answer lies with people. Technology can only assist.

57. Managers cannot learn from doing things right, only from doing them wrong.

Doing something right can only confirm what one already knows or believes; one cannot learn from it. However, one can learn from making mistakes, by identifying and correcting them. Nevertheless, making a mistake is frowned upon in most organizations, from school on up, and often is punishable. To the extent that recognition of mistakes is suppressed, so is learning.

There are two types of mistakes. Errors of commission consist of doing something that *should not* have been done. Errors of omission consist of not doing something that *should* have been done. Errors of omission are more serious than errors of commission because, among other reasons, they are often impossible or very difficult to correct. They are lost opportunities that can never be retrieved.

Organizations fail more often because of what they have not done than because of what they have done. (Similarly, it is worse to deny a truth than accept a falsehood.) But errors of omission are seldom recorded and accounted for. So, executives who cannot get away unpunished for doing something they should not have done, can usually get away with not doing something they should have done.

Since errors of commission are the only type of mistake accounted for, a security-seeking manager's optimal strategy is to avoid such errors by doing as little as possible, including nothing. The most successful executives are those who can create the appearance of doing a great deal without doing anything. Herein lies the root of an organization's disinclination to change.

We come back to the key to successful organisations: the ability and willingness to learn. Big leaps in growth and learning are accompanied by difficulty and pain. That's as true for individuals as it is for corporations. We don't tend to learn when we are toddling happily along. There is no reason for us to.

The opportunity for real and useful learning comes in the face of adversity. Some choose to take that opportunity; some don't. The latter keep on repeating the same mistakes their life over. For them, there is no chance of change as much as they say they want it. The same is true for organisations.

58. The principal objective of corporate executives is to provide themselves with the standard of living and quality of work life to which they aspire.

The maximization of shareholder value is alleged to be the principal objective of corporations. This illusion, propagated by executives, makes it possible to conceal their real objective: sustainable privilege.

Profit is a requirement, not an objective. As Peter Drucker once pointed out, profit is to a corporation what oxygen is to a human being: necessary for its existence, not a reason for it. Profit has absolutely no value to a corporation until it gets rid of it. This is also the case with many executives.

I agree. The majority of executives are still motivated not by shareholder value but by meeting their revenue and profit targets so that they can maximise their own pay and benefits. Some are certainly interested in increasing the standard and quality of their work life. Many will put up with substandard job quality as long as they are getting the money that gives them the trappings they want.

There are of course some senior executives who are genuinely driven by furthering the aims of the corporation. I would suggest though that they are not doing it for the sole purpose of creating shareholder value – that is a by-product. They are doing it because they want to develop and grow their business, leave a legacy, do the right thing. These are the rare ones. And creation of shareholder value is never a principal objective, either for the self-serving or for the right-minded.

59. The principal obstruction to an organization getting to where its managers most want it to be lies in the minds of its managers.

One can easily excuse oneself for not trying to get to where one wants to be: "They (or it) won't let me". Such attributions of blame are usually self-deceptions. The great American philosopher Pogo revealed the truth when he said, "We have met the enemy and he is us".

The fear of losing one's security and lack of self-confidence are the principal obstructions to progress — in other words, risk aversion. This lies inside, not outside, managers. There is no obstruction harder to recognize, let alone evade, than one that lies within oneself, largely because the content of one's mind is usually not visible to oneself.

In a changing environment, the future of an organization is generally determined more by what its management fails to do than by what it does. Organizational futures, or the lack thereof, are more often created by default than by deliberation.

There is an assumption here that managers want organisations to change. I would suggest that many more managers want things to stay the same than want them to change. They are comfortable: they are secure in what they know and they know that if they keep on doing what they do they will continue to get the pay and perks that go with the job. Except that if they don't change, the pay and the perks will disappear along with the business.

Change means uncertainty. Deciding to change takes courage. And it takes an inner confidence because by its very nature it threatens the status quo. True, those that get to the point of really wanting things to change must face the challenge of overcoming their own barriers before they can hope to overcome any other barriers. But no pain, no gain.

It's amazing how many so-called change agents think that everyone else should change except for themselves. Those that truly understand change and can bring it about in themselves and their organisations are those that have a high degree of self-awareness, sophisticated relationship skills and a real energy and motivation for change. An unusual package indeed.

60. A corporation's external boundaries are generally much more penetrable than its internal ones.

The competition for personal power and resources between managers and units within a corporation is often much more intense and less ethical than competition between corporations for customers.

Many managers act as though their performance, and hence their bonus, depends more on what their peers within the organization do, than on what their counterparts in other organizations do. And they believe their peers are "out to get them". Therefore, the information flow between peers is often less than it is between counterparts.

Improving communication between competing managers can often make things worse. As in war, the more each party knows about the other, the more harm they can do to each other. The problem is that with no information flowing between peers, the intensity of conflict between them decreases, but, unfortunately, so does organizational performance.

Herein lies a crucially important issue: that of collaboration versus hierarchy. Hierarchical structures encourage people to compete with each other rather than work together. They lead to people vying for the boss's attention; only doing what their position in the hierarchy allows; and focusing on internal politics not on the external world of competitors and customers.

Management consultants are hired in hierarchical organisations as they are needed to tell management 'how it is' because they rarely hear it from their own staff. Most CEOs hear what their staff think they want them to hear. In collaborative cultures there is a free flow of information, there is less fear and more honest communication: so such consultants are not needed.

What's more, collaborative ways of organising only work if there is a trust-based work culture where people share rather than compete. Trust is the core of the issue here. Without it the walls between the parts of a corporation will remain high. Useful communication can't take place without trust. Trust can't be built with the help of management consultants. Trust is a value. Values can't be manufactured.

In organisations with low-trust cultures the problem is not that competition is more intense within the organisation than between organisations, it's that managers focus their attention and energy internally not externally.

61. It is very difficult for those inside a box to think outside of it.

Those inside an organization, like those in Plato's cave, can only see shadows of things outside the organization. In addition, unlike those in Plato's cave, they often see only shadows of things inside the organization. Shadows are two-dimensional images of multi-dimensional reality; they fail to reflect the complexity of their source.

Shadows are determined by those who cast them, not by those who see them. They cannot be manipulated, but those who try often suffer from the illusion that they can be. An organization cannot control the future, but it can control a great deal of the effect of that future on it. The extent to which it can exercise such control depends on how well it can see the truth about itself.

It is very difficult for an organization to see the truth about itself. Those inside a box can seldom see what is happening within it. It usually takes someone looking from the outside in to produce useful evaluations.

A lot depends on how self-aware the organisation is – and on its culture. If it's a culture where senior executives are told only what they want to hear then those inside will be operating under delusions. If, however, honesty and truth telling are valued it's much more likely that a realistic self-view will exist.

Sometimes the most self-aware people are able to see and know much more about themselves than the objective outsider ever can. And that can apply to organisations too.

That leads to the other question: whether those inside the organisation want to see the truth or not. Often the most comfortable place to be is in total denial. It depends on the CEO and how much she wants to know what's really going on.

Having said all of that, even those organisations that have a realistic sense of themselves cannot possibly see themselves as outsiders could. It's always healthy and sensible to have an objective external view. Of course only those who are prepared to be challenged will do that. And that means asking the advice of those who are truly prepared to describe the naked state of the organisation. Otherwise there is no point. That raises the thorny issue of how an advisor or consultant is to recognise that a CEO is genuinely asking for critique because she is committed to change.

62. The level of organizational development is directly proportional to the size of the gap between where the organization is and where it wants to be.

Those who cannot think of a better state of affairs than the one they are in have no capacity for development. The smaller the gap between where an organization is and where it wants to be, the less developed it is. For example, restrictive, narrow-minded groups often cannot imagine a life much better than the one they have (except that they would like to undo recent changes in order to revert to a "golden age"). On the other hand, well-developed organizations and societies can think of many positive changes that would improve the quality of life they provide.

Continuous development requires: first, continuous unwillingness to settle for the state one is in however satisfying it may be; second, a conception of a better state; third, a way of pursuing it progressively that enables those doing so to extract satisfaction from the pursuit. Therefore, development requires both inspiration, the stimulation that induces the pursuit of something better, and recreation, the extraction of satisfaction from the pursuit itself.

Few organizations provide either.

Development does indeed require 'inspiration' and 'recreation'. It also requires ability. For individuals and organisations to change they must be able to change. All three elements must be present for it to work. Part of the ability is resilience; when things get tough and setbacks happen, resilience is needed to sustain momentum despite the difficulties.

We understand well how to make change happen, at least in theory. There are plenty of books and business school courses on the subject. Very few organisations manage to put the theory into practice though, because the combination of qualities needed to make change happen is rare. They cannot be injected into people. You can't just tell them what they need to do and then expect it to happen. They need to know how to change. But first they have to want to. The leader plays a key role in whether or not people want to.

Excellent leaders can inspire people with a vision of change. They have imagination. They can picture the future they want and they can make it compelling so that others want to follow. There are few such visionary leaders. Most people in charge of companies can only envisage incremental change. Even if they can see potential for larger change why would they take the necessary risks? No one was fired for playing safe. Many a CEO has been fired for taking too big a risk.

63. Most stated, corporate objectives are platitudes – they say nothing, but hide this fact behind words.

Many alleged statements have no content, say nothing. For example, "Too much alcohol (or anything) is bad for you." This is a platitude; perhaps the worst kind, a tautology. A tautology is a statement that asserts that something is itself. (Sic!) Can you imagine asserting that "Too much alcohol is good for you."? Of course not, because "too much" means "an amount that is bad for you."

Therefore, the statement "Too much alcohol is bad for you" is equivalent to "An amount of alcohol that is bad for you is bad for you." Motherhood statements are also platitudes. They are statements the negative of which would never be asserted by a reasonable person, let alone a manager.

For example, "We should provide our stockholders with an adequate return on their investments." Can you imagine anyone asserting that a corporation shouldn't do this? Unless the negative of an assertion is sensible, the positive version cannot be.

Most stated corporate objectives put to this test would dissolve.

One of the most common platitudes in today's corporations is 'we value our people'. The sentiment is great, but if they really value their people why do they need to state it?

Experience tells us whether or not a statement is a platitude. We believe someone more if they live what they say rather than tell it. Having said that, those that really live something want to find a short way to express it – because they think it's important. As such, platitudes are often a shortcut – instead of writing several paragraphs about exactly how they value their people they just say 'we value our people'.

So, the advantage of platitudes is that they're concise; the disadvantage is that they may have lost all meaning. All the more so if the platitude is tautological!

The test you suggest is a good one. Another example is: 'our customers matter'. What you're pointing to is that these statements need qualification; they aren't simple. So: 'our customers matter because, unless they buy our products, we'll go out of business', or, 'we need to make enough profit to keep our shareholders happy so they don't sell up'. Honesty might be a better policy sometimes. And let's not forget that if a company asks shareholders to suspend reward in order for the company to survive in the short-term and flourish in the long-term, many shareholders will jump ship.

64. Most corporations and business schools are less than the sum of their parts.

The break-up value of most business schools and corporations is greater than their value as a whole. This follows from the fact that one of their core competencies is their ability to prevent productive interactions between their parts. They obstruct each other and this results in negative synergy.

In corporations as in business schools, negative synergy is a consequence of disapproval, if not punishment, of those who cross departmental lines. Those who do so are believed to be disloyal to their department and to be prostituting their competence.

The strength of an individual's loyalty is usually greatest when applied to the smallest organizational unit of which that individual is a part. It decreases as the size of the containing units increase. Thus, one's greatest loyalty is to oneself; one's smallest loyalty is to humankind.

In some corporations it may still be true that those who cross departmental lines are thought disloyal. But a growing number are encouraging employees to do just that because they know the importance of collaboration. Take the case of a corporation that's trying to grow by cross selling its products. It relies on its sales people sharing leads and making joint pitches.

People feel loyalty to a cause or a person they value not to a department unless that department is representative of the thing they care about. It's necessary to understand the reason for the loyalty in order to know whether it's really valuable. Some are loyal in a sycophantic sense. Others are loyal because they genuinely believe in something or someone. They are the ones who are committed and passionate and do what they can to further the cause.

So it's not the size of the department upon which the amount of loyalty shown by an employee depends. The many 'Best Companies to work for' league tables show that some very large companies have a high rate of employee loyalty. These days loyalty is not as easy for companies to earn as it was in the old days when a decent salary and benefits were enough. People today expect and want more from their work. They want meaning, satisfaction and recognition. Of course loyalty is only one component of productive working. Whether or not an organisation is more than the sum of its parts depends on much more than where the loyalties lie.

65. Managers who try to make themselves look good by making others look bad, look worse than those they try to make look bad.

It is easier to make others fail than to help them succeed. Therefore, it is easier for subordinates to make their superiors fail than to help them succeed. Enmity begets enmity; cooperation begets cooperation. In order for managers to rise in a hierarchy over the remains of others, they must receive the cooperation of the others they have damaged on the way up. They are unlikely to get it.

To be elevated because of one's own competence is better than elevation because of the apparent incompetence of others. A great deal more can be accomplished with the help of competent others than with the absence of help from incompetent others. Therefore, one of the best ways for managers to help themselves is to help to increase the competence of their subordinates and their peers.

It's true that such managers make themselves look bad. But most people like that tend to be canny and those who have the power over them rarely notice what they are doing, so it doesn't affect their career opportunities.

It very much depends on the organisational environment. I don't know many companies where support of subordinates is critical to the promotion opportunities of the bosses. In fact, quite the opposite. Those who take decisions about who gets on in a company don't take account of what the subordinate staff think. Sure the staff can affect the success of the manager by deliberately producing substandard work or providing defective information. That is unlikely though because they will damage themselves in the process.

Decisions about who should be elevated in an organisation are rarely logical. The best person very often doesn't get the job. That's because decisions are too often based on who makes the boss feel more comfortable, who challenges the least, who toes the line, not who would be the best performer.

66. The morality that many managers espouse in public is inversely proportional to the morality they practice in private.

Be wary of those who berate the morality of others and celebrate their own in public. One's own morality does not require reinforcement by attacking the immorality of others. Morality is its own reward; it does not require the awareness, approval, admiration, or financial support of others. Immorality does.

Those who preach virtue publicly and pretend to practice it are trying either to conceal their own sins, or to make a living off the sins of others.

Overt moralists greatly resent the fun others have from behaving immorally. Perhaps the reason they do not practice the morality they preach is that they do not know how to have fun morally.

Those who try to convince others of their morality are likely to be greeted with mistrust by others. When senior executives sit down to decide what they want their company's values to be then they are badly missing the point. Values, like morality, just are. They should be asking themselves what their values are, not what values they want. Morality and values are deeply ingrained from early childhood. Most people don't acquire new ones, and if they do it's usually a means to an end.

There is, of course, a difference between 'overt moralists' and those who have their own authentic morality. Public moralists have pseudo values only. Worse, they preach them to others. They talk the talk but don't walk the walk.

67. The higher their rank, the less managers perceive a need for continuing education, but the greater their need for it.

The pretension to omniscience increases with rank and it does so with decreasing justification. In general, the more senior the managers, the more open their mouths and the more closed their minds.

The only way to get senior executives to attend a course is to hold it in the Bahamas on a golf course and have them bring their wives or a reasonable facsimile thereof. The educational part of a senior executive course must be restricted to no more than a few hours per day, with attendance optional. The course must also be very costly. Its value is judged to be directly proportional to its cost, its distance from home, and its exclusion of those of lower rank.

The most popular presenters are managerial evangelists and panacea peddlers. They are evaluated more by the energy they exert than the enlightenment they spread, by the excitement they induce rather than the inspiration they provide.

 Unfortunately, most evangelists and panacea peddlers can propagate trivia more convincingly than most educators can transmit knowledge, understanding or wisdom.

So true! A glossy looking course in a sexy location with confident and charismatic facilitators can be the worst load of tripe ever and get great ratings. It's about entertainment and ego preservation. It's not about learning.

Unfortunately many of those who genuinely do have something to teach aren't good at packaging it to encourage executives to attend. Those who are great at packaging tend not to be too interested in whether their participants learn anything, just whether they ticked the right boxes on the 'happy sheets'.

68. The number of references and citations in a book is inversely proportional to the amount of thinking the author has done.

The number of citations is often used as a basis for estimating the knowledge of the author. Nothing could be a less reliable guide. The number of references and citations is directly proportional to the amount of thinking of others he/she has used. Most allegedly learned books are nothing but compilations of other peoples' learning, carefully organized and presented so as to be less comprehensible than the originals.

Appropriate and approved citations are what give a book legitimacy. For example, any book on management that does not cite Peter Drucker immediately brands the author as illiterate. Authors are not expected to have read Drucker but they are expected to feel guilty if they haven't.

The more often an author refers to him/herself is proportional to the extent that the current writing repeats what he/she has previously written.

And I thought it was the British who were famed for their cynicism! An author who cites lots of other authors could also be someone who makes connections, is widely read and wants to credit the others for contributing to their own knowledge and/or inspiring them.

The most interesting and insightful writings can be those in books and weblogs that bring others' thinking into play. Referring to others' works shows an open-mindedness and confidence. It shows that someone is genuinely interested in acquiring and spreading knowledge and acknowledges the contributions of others in this process. Personally I enjoy this type of writing as it gives me the perspectives of others not just the author. It makes the experience more rounded.

As Malcolm Gladwell, the author of **Blink**, once said, he never knows whether his thoughts are original because they are inevitably a combination of what he has read and been told as well as his own original angles on the world. So in citing Gladwell, I may also be referencing some, if not several, other authors!

69. No computer is smarter than those who program it. Those who program computers are seldom smarter than those who try to use their output.

Therefore, the computer has become a very efficient way of distributing ignorance and inefficiency. It is extremely efficient in consuming time unproductively, but in a challenging and entertaining way. Trying to prove that a person is smarter than the computer is an entertaining way of getting nothing done.

There is only one thing a computer can do that a person can't do: remember a forecast without changing it. Of course it can do many things faster than a person, especially wrong things.

Computers cannot use people nearly as well as people can use computers. A great deal more can be done by people without computers than by computers without people. Computers amplify man's incapabilities; they do not replace them. They cannot distinguish between right and wrong, good and evil, or beauty and ugliness.

Information and knowledge can be entered into a computer, but not understanding and wisdom. However rare understanding and wisdom are among humans, they are not to be found at all in computers. Technology is neither good nor evil, but it enhances man's inclination toward both.

Computers and computer-driven gadgets are so ubiquitous today that it seems bizarre to talk about them as though there is much choice whether to use them. Our homes, our offices, our cars, our entire lives are full of them.

Of course they are only as good as the designer and the user but that is true of any technological invention. It's odd to even think along the lines of whether the computer is better than us. In some ways it is, in some it isn't. It's probably more useful to think about how computer technology has enhanced our lives, made them easier and more exciting. The computer and the intelligent and moral human being are an extremely powerful combination.

For example, a friend I admire greatly spent a deal of time the other day composing a blog on the way computers and the Internet have given us an easy way to put across our ideas. Of course, it was on company time and his PC never did get back to him.

70. Managers cannot talk and listen at the same time; in fact, most managers find it very difficult to listen even when they are not talking.

Some consider this to be the most serious defect possible in the design of managers. It is bad enough that they cannot hear what others are saying, but they do not even hear themselves. This prevents them from doing unto themselves as they do unto others. Managers talk to or at their subordinates to avoid having to listen to them or themselves.

Hearing and listening are not the same thing. To hear another is to know that they are saying something without knowing what they are saying. Knowing what they are saying requires listening. Hearing is done with the ears; listening is done with the mind; listening is minding what others have to say. One must have a mind to listen; ears are not enough. Failure to listen results in atrophy of the mind.

IT IS DIFFICULT To HEAR WHEN Talking

There is a serious reason for managers not listening. It has to do with a refusal to hear anything that does not accord with their existing views. They just want their own model of the world reinforced – over and over again. Only managers who are interested in doing things better are interested in listening.

The inability to listen and learn is a natural by-product of hierarchical management structures and institutionalised power. Those lower down the hierarchy are less powerful, so there is little benefit in listening to them. Although some companies have feedback processes – inviting questions and views from staff at different hierarchical levels – this is usually done for the feel-good factor. It gives the pretence of listening and gives those at the top the perfect disguise behind which to mould the messages they want to get across to their employees.

The bottom line is that if management hears anything that it would rather not hear it is discounted. The worst consequence of this is perhaps even worse than mental atrophy. It can be fatal, as in the Challenger Space Shuttle tragedy when it didn't suit NASA management to listen to the engineers who said the mission should be aborted for safety reasons. What followed was indeed a disaster. Afterwards, management felt it had even more reason to refuse to listen to the engineers. It had to eliminate all dissent and the person who spoke up was fired.

71. Overheads, slides and PowerPoint projectors are *not* visual aids to managers. They transform managers into auditory aids to the visuals.

Black, white and green boards and easels-and-pads are visual aids, but slide, overhead and PowerPoint projectors are not. They eliminate the need for the speaker to think while talking. The speaker is frequently viewed as an obstruction to reading what is projected.

In general, the more artistic projections are, the less significant is their content. Copies of slides or overheads distributed beforehand eliminate the need for members of the audience to pay attention to the speaker and remove any guilt they might feel by not doing so. This is not altered by the fact that the handouts are seldom used after the presentation. Their principal function is to provide evidence of attendance. They also provide those in the audience with something to occupy their minds while the speaker drones on.

In addition, a speaker who reads what is on the screen insults a literate audience unless he or she had the foresight to make the projections illegible or incomprehensible.

Agreed. PowerPoint is an overused tool. Instead of using it to enhance their presentations many managers use it as a crutch, a way to make sure they remember what they're going to say and a focal point that takes their audience's attention away from them.

If a presenter is skilled and persuasive it doesn't matter what type of visual aid he uses, he will influence the audience. If he isn't then he'll bore the audience no matter what he does.

Good presenters tell a story, using the Emotional Intelligence skills of empathy and affect to establish a rapport and build a connection with their audience. Before PowerPoint was invented people tried harder to develop these skills. Technology disables people and communication just as often as it enables them. Technology like PowerPoint helps managers forget that they are talking to human beings who actually need to be engaged and who listen more when they can respond emotionally to a presenter.

This is a reminder that the best organisations almost always put emphasis on interpersonal skills.

72. Conversations in a lavatory are more productive than those in the boardroom.

An informal conversation while "using the facilities" is often more productive than a long, stifling, formal meeting. There is unlikely to be posturing or political infighting at such a time and place. And what is being passed is not the time of day.

Women managers are at a disadvantage because of the difference in the physical layout of men's and women's restrooms. This is not likely to change but women's behavior in their facilities is likely to. Perhaps installing intra-cubicle communication equipment (auditory, not visual) would help.

Women will have to learn that privacy is not nearly as important as the ability to converse without constraints.

It depends what men and women talk about in the lavatory. If what they talk about in other settings is indicative then men's talk will be transactional, superficial and about 'things'. In other words, nothing too threatening for conversation when in a vulnerable state. Women, on the other hand, when we relate, we relate. We tend to have two-way dialogue rather than two separate monologues. We tend to listen more, empathise more and talk about ideas and feelings not just things. It's more intimate and we're more connected with the person we're relating to. This kind of conversation doesn't lend itself to the kind of setting where you're divided into separate cubicles.

It's men who need to learn the ability to converse without constraints, not women. Of course the setting is important – the more informal it is the more it encourages open dialogue. Casual exchanges and sharing of information may well happen in the lavatory but matters of importance that need privacy can't be discussed there.

73. To managers an ounce of wisdom is worth a pound of understanding.

This makes an ounce of wisdom worth 65,536 ounces of data, using the following formula:

1oz wisdom = 1lb understanding
1oz understanding = 1lb knowledge
1oz knowledge = 1lb information
1oz information = 1lb data

Wisdom is contained in value statements, for example, aphorisms and proverbs. It enables us to perceive and evaluate the long-term as well as short-term consequences of what we do. It induces us to want to pursue things of lasting value. It enables us to make short-run sacrifices for long-run gains. It prevents our sacrificing the future for the present.

Knowledge enables us to make things work; understanding enables us to make things work the way we want; wisdom enables us to want the "right" things, things that increase our ability to obtain what we and others need and want.

Information, knowledge, and understanding enable us to do things right, to be efficient, but wisdom enables us to do the right things, to be effective. Science pursues data, information, knowledge, and understanding: what is truth; but the humanities pursue wisdom: what is right.

It's true that many managers in today's corporates would rather do things right than do the right thing. They either don't have the ability or the desire to thoroughly understand an issue and its implications.

It goes without saying that wisdom requires a certain intelligence as well as a strong moral motivation. But it also takes courage. To be courageous you must rise above the politics and personal agendas of organisations and push the right decisions through. It's not at all obvious that the wise always act on their wisdom though. There are many wise people in companies who decide not to question the status quo. Wise people who act on their wisdom often take risks in doing so because they are going against the tide. So courage is a key in the wisdom-completing process.

There are plenty of managers who have knowledge and understanding. There are few examples of wise leaders in the corporate world.

74. The press is the sword of Damocles that hangs over the head of every organization.

Press is a verb, not a noun. What it does is scare the hell out of executives that care more about what others think of them, particularly security analysts, than what they think of themselves.

Press coverage that is favorable is always considered to be accurate; but unfavorable coverage is always taken to be a clear distortion of the truth by a biased reporter who is ill informed, corrupt, prejudiced, and feeble minded.

To a large extent the press has come to supplement the alleged system of justice; it determines the guilt or innocence of alleged criminal or immoral acts even before they are judged in court and, in some cases, even before they are committed. It often convicts the innocent long before the alleged justice system does.

Unfortunately, it also often liberates the guilty long before the justice system does. Unlike declarations made by the criminal justice system, allegations made by the press are seldom revocable.

Even the most respected press often gives a distorted view of what is going on. The least respected press always gives a distorted view of what is not going on.

The positive thing about the press is that it can hold organisations and their CEOs accountable in a way that shareholders can't or don't. It's one of the few truly powerful checks and balances that exist for organisations and it's important that it's allowed freedom.

Journalists tend to be individualistic and independent minded. In democratic countries they tend not to worry about writing what they believe is true or exposing what they believe needs to be exposed. Of course there are those who would say that the press is less free in the USA than in the UK (Watergate notwithstanding), and that corporations have far too much influence on it.

I relish the power of the press to monitor the way organisations go about their business and would prefer to see the independence of the press strengthened. Like everything else, the press should be regulated openly, in court, rather than by the prejudice of media owners and by government pressure.

Perhaps the only way not to fear the press is to be open and transparent and prepared to argue one's corner.

75. The more managers try to get rid of what they don't want, the less likely they are to get what they do want.

When one gets rid of what one does not want, one is likely to get something one wants even less. When DDT was used to get rid of pests it harmed things we did not want to harm. Prohibition brought a stimulus to organized crime that was much more harmful to society than abuse of alcohol.

The US has the highest percentage of its population in prison and one of the highest crime rates in the world. Yet studies show that, on release, a prisoner is more likely to commit a crime than before going into prison; and the resulting crime is likely to be more serious.

It is more difficult to define what we want than to point at what we do not want. Nevertheless, a "getting rid of" strategy is a cop out. Great gains are seldom made easily.

Managers should know at all times what they would have if they could have anything they wanted. The most effective way to do this is through idealized design. This involves a redesign of the organization on the assumption that it was destroyed last night. The only constraints are that the design must be technologically feasible and able to survive in the current environment. Then, the most effective way of creating the future is by reducing the gap between the current state and the result of the idealized design.

Getting rid of what you don't want *is* an effective strategy for getting what one wants in life in general. In order to move away from what we don't want we have to spend time paying attention to it. Otherwise our attention will be constantly dragged back to what we are trying to avoid. Much more effective however is to become clear what we do want. In that, this f-Law is correct. It's a sequence thing. Know what you want, get rid of what you don't want – the latter being part of the process of 'reducing the gap'.

A classic example of getting rid of things before you know what you want in organisations is in the area of training and development. Companies spend a lot of time and training budget trying to fix people's weaknesses. An example of this is how much effort goes into trying to make managers out of people who don't have the aptitude and, more importantly, the motivation to be a manager. It's far more effective to spend time focusing through the positive in developing what people are already good at and motivated to do. But, of course, you're right, it would be even more effective to select the right people in the first place. Again that means knowing what you want in the first place.

76. Focusing on an organization's "core competency" diverts attention from its core competencies.

In a rapidly changing business environment, such as we have, the most important competencies are (1) the readiness, willingness, and ability to change, and (2) the ability to innovate. The absence of these competencies is more likely to result in failure than the presence of other competencies is to assure success.

However well an organization does what it currently does, it will not survive unless it learns both how to do the old things better and new things well. The ability to learn and adapt is the most important core competency an organization can have. Unfortunately, these abilities are in very short supply. Making the best horse-drawn carriage in the world did not enable its manufacturer to survive the automobile.

The average life of an American corporation has been estimated to be as low as eleven and a half years. The failures are due much more to what organizations cannot do than to what they can.

I've made the point throughout our conversation that the lack of ability to learn and change is a real problem in organisations. It stems from the fact that (a) we don't learn how to learn at school (b) companies don't realise how important learning is.

In schools we're taught how to be taught, how to acquire knowledge and how to pass exams. We don't learn the skills of learning: self-awareness, listening, reflection and personal change. So we grow up and join organisations where all the others have been taught the same thing. No one is learning. Everyone goes round doing things in the same way over and over.

The term 'the learning organisation' only really caught on in academic circles. It was too much of a step for executives to take on board. Organisations will continue to have short life spans and/or stunted growth until they understand the importance of learning for growth.

You could be forgiven for thinking that executives won't get the message because they're too busy explaining to shareholders why what they are doing is right. Their attention is on that, not on learning. Learning involves risk. Executives don't like risk – especially personal risk that opens them up to criticism. Taking risks can get them fired, doing what has always proved successful in the past can't.

77. The greater the fee paid to corporate directors, the less their contributions are likely to be.

If a director's participation on a corporate board depends on how much it pays him/her, he/she is generally more interested in the pay than the organization. He/she is then often in the pocket of the CEO, operates as a rubber stamp, and expects the same in return – organizational incest.

A director should have two functions: to represent the interests of the corporation's external stakeholders, and to represent the corporation to them. In the first of these functions a director must serve as a constructive critic of corporate behavior and assure the corporation's exercise of social responsibility. A director cannot perform this function if payment for his/her services depends on the extent to which he/she supports the CEO, no matter what. A good corporate board is not the CEO's board but the CEO is the board's chief of staff. It is a board to which the CEO is beholden, not one whose members are beholden to the CEO.

The reason that directors often find it difficult to undertake the role (a legitimate one) of corporate critic is not just to do with the fact that they are being paid and may be in the CEO's pocket. The same thing happens in schools – governors don't get paid, some are not in the Headteacher's pocket, but it's probably relatively rare for them to challenge the way the school is run even if they think it needs challenging.

These sorts of social structures tend to encourage the maintenance of the status quo rather than challenge it. Any challenge there is, is a pseudo challenge. In these situations, people are operating in a power structure. Even though the CEO and the Headteacher are supposed to be accountable to the stakeholders they tend to support their sponsors. The only way to create a system where there can be a genuine challenge is to remove the challengers from the power structure altogether. Keep them outside but give them some power. It would really help if they were held accountable in reality as well as in theory.

Of course there are those who do the job well and do hold their sponsors to account. These types tend not to stay in the job long and it's remarkable that they ever got there in the first place.

78. A manager's fear of computers is directly proportional to the square of his/her age.

Pre-computer-age managers act as though personal computers bite and are very fragile. Children who have no such misconceptions learn how to use computers instinctively. They have the further advantage of not being able to read the instructions on their use.

Intelligent seniors learn not to use a computer without immediate access to a preschool youngster. If they try to go it alone, they are likely to get caught in a Web.

The inability to use a computer is as prevalent among adults as the inability to use a book is among youngsters. This greatly magnifies the difficulty of communication between generations.

Adults who use computers to generate conclusions tend to blame the computers for any errors that result. This is like blaming one's hand for one's illegible handwriting.

Nevertheless, most adults come to like computers because their downtimes provide more free time than holidays.

This fear is not so much to do with age as to the attitude to learning and change. There are those who will always embrace the latest technology and new ways of doing things because that's the sort of people they are. And then there are those who will resist and hang on to their usual ways of doing things.

If someone is open to change in one aspect of life he or she tends to be open to change in others. I know 60 year-olds who are way more computer-savvy than some people in their 30s. Moreover they tend not to like the downtimes but would never take their laptops with them on holiday.

79. Most managers know less about managing people than the conductor of an orchestra does.

Unlike a manager, the conductor of an orchestra does not tell his subordinates how to play their instruments, but how to play together. Most, if not all, members of an orchestra can play their instruments better than the conductor can. So it would be stupid as well as insulting for the conductor to instruct them on how to play their instruments. The conductor's job is not to manage their actions, but their interactions; not to supervise but to coordinate and integrate.

However, interactions can only be optimized when each individual knows how each of the others is performing. An orchestra in which none of the players could hear what the other players are doing would be cacophonous. In addition, they must have a common objective, one score to play.

Without a manager who focuses on interactions, who sees to it that each subordinate has the information about the others they require, and makes sure that all subordinates have a common objective, there can be no harmony.

Mgr. conducting a cacophony

What's more, members of an orchestra <u>want</u> to play together. They are motivated to work together to produce the end result. They need each other to achieve something that none of them can achieve alone.

In practice, at work people are seldom highly motivated to work together. Results require motivation plus skill. As well as having the skill, musicians are usually highly motivated. They are doing what they love to do. For many it's a calling. For most people in most organisations that is not the case. Leaders need to find out what motivates people. A tough question, as most people don't know that even about themselves. They need to agree goals that everyone is wholeheartedly committed to and they need to support the team to deliver its best performance.

So, the conductor has it easy in comparison. A leader's job is much tougher.

80. Complex problems do not have simple solutions, only simple minded managers and their consultants think they do.

Panaceas in good currency prevail despite disconfirming evidence. They prevail until one alleged to be better comes along. Therefore, gullible managers ride a yo-yo manipulated by consultants and academics who produce and peddle panaceas.

The only problems that have simple solutions are simple problems. The only managers that have simple problems have simple minds. Problems that arise in organizations are almost always the product of interactions of parts, never the action of a single part. Complex problems do not have simple solutions.

Complexity is not a property of problems but of those looking at problems. Any problem that we know how to solve is simple; any that we don't is complex.

Familiarity breeds complexity. This is why the problems confronted by others, with which we have little or no familiarity, always appear to be simpler than the ones we confront ourselves.

People want simplicity. It's easier to deal with than complexity. Business book sales are falling. The ones doing best are those that promise 'Seven easy steps to…' or 'The six habits of…', etc. Further evidence of an appetite for quick and easy panaceas?

The worrying thing is the effect on children's education. We're breeding an easy-answer, sound-bite generation. They don't want to engage in complex debate, philosophising and struggling with complex questions. They want quick, easy and instant. We see it not only in the types of books that sell but in the sales of tabloid papers and in dumbed-down TV programming.

Engaging with a complex problem, philosophising with colleagues, struggling, as mathematicians do, to solve a riddle, can all be deeply satisfying. Human beings need meaning in their lives. Great leaders encourage people to find meaning in what they do. But the majority of managers don't. They want easy answers. Those that prosper over the long term and find satisfaction in doing it are those who are prepared to engage with the complex problems. Sadly, this is a small elite.

There is hope. At least these days the small elite can find each other via the Internet. This could be a sign that the 'quick and easy' answer brigade is being balanced out by the 'we know there are no easy answers but want to explore' brigade. Maybe!

81. When nothing can make things worse, anything can make them better.

When corporate executives are asked, "How are things?" they occasionally answer, "They couldn't be worse". What a wonderful position to be in! If this is true, then nothing can be done to make things "worser". Therefore, such a statement implies that doing anything would probably make things better. It is a time to act.

The couldn't-be-worse situation is, in one sense, much better for an organization than one about which it is said, "It couldn't be better". Nevertheless, this latter is an evaluation executives much prefer. If it is true, however, doing anything in such a state would only make it worse. This is a worse situation than one in which doing anything can make it better. The claim that things could not be better absolves executives of the need to do anything except gloat.

There are weaker assertions that are equally effective at discouraging action: for example, "Things may not be perfect but they are good enough", "Don't rock the boat", "Let well enough alone" or "Let nature take its course."

There is nothing as absolute as absolving oneself of the need to do something, anything. Such absolution eliminates any sense of guilt and, therefore, the need for confession.

A cynic might suggest that waiting until things couldn't be worse is an effective strategy for change management because it drives executives to action. And action is something that many executives shy away from.

Indeed it can take near disaster to drive corporations into action. Think of IBM or Marks and Spencer. It wasn't until their platforms were on fire that they woke up to the fact that they were in real danger of going out of business. It had to be that serious before they would act.

I'm reminded of the management theory proposed by Taiichi Ohno, the father of lean manufacturing: when a company is facing disaster, the situation will generate the kind of radical, creative thinking that isn't otherwise possible.

It used to be thought that management should artificially generate crises to provoke a dramatic response. With the speed of change facing almost every organisation these days, it seems we don't need to generate them any more. The next crisis is always just around the corner.

The Authors

Russell L. Ackoff is the Anheuser-Busch Emeritus Professor of Management Science at the University of Pennsylvania. He has authored 22 books on Systems Management, the most recent of which are: *Beating the System*, co-authored with Sheldon Rovin and published by Berrett-Kohler; *Re-Designing the Corporation*, published by Oxford University Press and *Ackoff's Best*, published by Wiley. A founding member of the Institute of Management Sciences, his work in consulting and education has involved more than 350 corporations and 75 government agencies in the States and beyond. Management grandee, he was ranked 26 in the recent list of top business brains in the world, in *The Times*.

Herbert J. Addison has worked for some 40 years in academic, educational and business book publishing. He is the author of the business section in the *New York Times Guide to Essential Knowledge*. Addison and Ackoff, who are close friends, have undertaken several collaborative projects, most recently co-authoring *Idealized Design: Creating an Organization's Future*, published by Wharton School Publishing.

Sally Bibb is Director, Group Sales Development for the Economist Group and is based in London with responsibility for Europe, Asia and North America. She has specialised in organization and executive development for 15 years and has a Masters Degree in Organisational Change. Co-author of award-winning book *Trust Matters — for organisational and personal success* published by Palgrave MacMillan; she is series editor for the 'Truths about Business' series published by Marshall Cavendish/Cyan and author of *The Stone Age Company: why the companies we work for are dying and how they can saved*, the first in the series.

About Triarchy Press

Triarchy Press is a new publishing house that looks at how organizations work and how to make them work better. We aim to present challenging perspectives on organizations in short, pithy but rigorously argued books.

Through our books, e-publications and discussion area, we aim to stimulate ideas by encouraging real debate about organizations in partnership with people who work in, research or just like to think about them.

Visit our website to:
- submit your own ƒ-Law
- buy copies of this book or **A Little Book of f-Laws**
- find out about ordering larger quantities of personalised copies of either book for your organization
- get free access to our library of articles
- find out about Triarchy Press events and seminars
- join the debate in our discussion forum
- submit a book proposal

www.f-laws.com

www.triarchypress.com

Breinigsville, PA USA
25 January 2010

231328BV00002B/1/A